What people are saying about …

Passport through Darkness

"What you read in this book will be used of God to motivate you to action on behalf of vulnerable children around the world. In the process, as you walk with Kimberly, you may also find perspective, forgiveness, and healing in your own life. May God use His servant's story to His glory. Not only Kimberly's story, but yours and mine as well."

From the foreword by Randy Alcorn,
best-selling author of *Heaven* and *If God Is Good*

"What I love about this book is that it's a real-life story filled with credibility from a friend. It isn't an idea—it's a reality. Read this, and then do it."

Dr. Bob Roberts, Jr., senior pastor
at NorthWood Church

"Kimberly Smith has seen the desperation and powerlessness of people caught up in the struggle for life and survival. Her experiences in Darfur bring home the bruta'_____ r and the indifference of the worlc _____ e of this book is not despair but hc _____ c God forgives and renews and tha _____ hopeless situations in life and draws us into truth.

Dr. Elaine Storkey, author, broadcaster, president
of Tearfund, and ambassador for Restored

"A literary treasure … this book will shock and intrigue you and open your eyes to consider more courageous avenues in serving God and suffering humankind than ever before. Kimberly Smith weaves her story of ultimate human love, hate, and forgiveness balanced between home and hell. She risks all to give voice to victims of unimaginable cruelty, and in doing so, she exposes herself to that same darkness."

Linda C. Fuller, cofounder of Habitat for Humanity International and the Fuller Center for Housing

"Kimberly Smith has been a Mother Teresa to the people of Sudan. She rescues suffering girls and lost boys forgotten by everyone but God."

Greg Garrison, reporter for *The Birmingham News*

"*Passport through Darkness* is the extraordinary life journey of Kimberly Smith, an incredible woman with a passion to accomplish the unimaginable! And she succeeds! An amazing story and inspiring read."

Denise George, speaker and author of twenty-five books, including *The Secret Holocaust Diaries*

"I dare you to read this book! You will be wrecked by God's call, humanity's cry, and a subsequent move to action. The honesty and gravity of this book will bring personal healing, compassion, and a calibration of heart. This book has become recommended reading for our students and workers in the nations."

Riaan Heyns, pastor of Global
Ministries at New Life Church

"This is more than a well-written, powerful, and inspiring story. It is a change agent that will impact the way you see abused and abandoned children. More importantly, the author allows you to look beyond individual heroic acts of ministry and see the spiritual journey of a soul who has an emerging passion for God. It is not only a telescope that shows you what is occurring in the Sudan but also a microscope that will help you look into your own heart. This book is contagious."

Dr. Gary Fenton, senior pastor at Dawson Family
of Faith and Dawson Memorial Baptist Church

"I finished reading this book several weeks ago and yet the message has haunted me almost every day since. Kimberly's story of her many trials and triumphs in the Sudan is both heart-wrenching and inspiring. The book reads like the most adventurous, power-packed drama of all time … and yet it is true! I couldn't put this book down."

Donna Schuller, CNC, pastor and author of *A
Legacy of Success* and *Woman to Woman Wisdom*

"Angelina Jolie she's not. She's not a martial arts expert or a small-arms expert or an expert in—well—*anything*. She has no classified files in her past, no shadowy backstory in special ops, and her only brush with international intrigue was once squinting in a dark theater at the subtitles of a foreign film. She is, in fact, a soft-spoken Southern woman with fair skin prone to burning and red hair prone to frizzing. Hardly a casting director's dream for the role in the story you are about to read, she's far too uncomfortable as a leading lady, far too unsure of herself, far too tormented by her inner fears. However, she was *God's* dream for the role. I recently read a book on story, where the author said that the greatest stories aren't about undaunted characters who overcome their greatest foes but about unlikely characters who overcome their greatest fears. Kimberly Smith is one of those characters. And *this* is one of those stories."

Ken Gire, author of *Moments with the Savior,*
Windows of the Soul, and *The North Face of God*

"From her camp in the desert Kimberly L. Smith pulls back the canvas of her tent to show us the good, the bad, and the ugly of our world today in *Passport through Darkness.* She allows us to see into her 'tent of meeting' (Ex. 33:7) with God. The level of transparency and intimacy she reveals in her walk with God and her husband is encouraging, inspiring, motivating, and challenging. This book challenges Westerners about their contentment with insulated 'secure' lives—as we sit and sing our polite little songs in our pristine churches. How do we not stand up for our brothers and sisters thousands of miles away where human beings are treated without dignity—trafficked, bought, sold, and traded like animals?"

Tomi Lee "T. L." Grover, PhD, anti-trafficking
consultant and founder of www.TraffickStop.org

"If I didn't know Kimberly well, I would have thought she was writing fiction. *Passport through Darkness* is real, raw, full of vulnerability—and is infused with much hope and love. But I do know Kimberly well, and I know that she has experienced the darkest sides of humanity—and the brightest piercings of the light of God's redemptive love. Reading this book will propel us all beyond our self-imposed boundaries, to the ultimate risk of finding and following Christ's call for our own lives."

Rev. Dr. Lauran Bethell, global consultant, Ministries with Victims of Human Trafficking and Prostitution, International Ministries, ABC/ USA; coordinator, International Christian Alliance on Prostitution; and former director, New Life Center, Chiang Mai, Thailand

"In the song 'Amazing Grace,' the songwriter rejoices that he was once blind but now he sees. Because of some horrific, dangerous, and miraculous experiences, Kimberly Smith definitely sees the world with new eyes. As she struggles to help orphan and rape victims survive, she goes deep inside places that most Westerners barely glimpse on the evening news. But Kimberly proves that once your eyes have been opened you can never be the same again. This book will surely open your eyes to the plight that befalls women and children around the world, but more than that, it provides evidence that in the midst of suffering is where you truly discover God and His greatness."

Dr. Tom White, executive director of Voice of the Martyrs–USA

PASSPORT
THROUGH
DARKNESS

A True Story of Danger
and Second Chances

KIMBERLY L. SMITH

David C Cook®
transforming lives together

PASSPORT THROUGH DARKNESS
Published by David C Cook
4050 Lee Vance View
Colorado Springs, CO 80918 U.S.A.

David C Cook Distribution Canada
55 Woodslee Avenue, Paris, Ontario, Canada N3L 3E5

David C Cook U.K., Kingsway Communications
Eastbourne, East Sussex BN23 6NT, England

The graphic circle C logo is a registered trademark of David C Cook.

All Scripture quotations are taken from *The Holy Bible, English Standard Version*. Copyright © 2000; 2001 by Crossway Bibles, a division of Good News Publishers. Used by permission. All rights reserved.

Some names have been changed for privacy purposes.

LCCN 2010939815
ISBN 978-1-4347-0212-8
eISBN 978-1-4347-0302-6

© 2011 Kimberly L. Smith
Published in association with the literary agency of WordServe Literary
Group, Ltd., 10152 S. Knoll Circle, Highlands Ranch, CO 80130

The Team: Terry Behimer, Susan Tjaden, Sarah Schultz, Jack Campbell, Karen Athen
Cover Design: Amy Kiechlin
Cover Photo: iStockphoto

Printed in the United States of America

First Edition 2011

3 4 5 6 7 8 9 10

022712

For Dellanna O'Brien
1933–2008
Thank you for the fire of bravery and gentleness you lived,
and continue to spark within us.
I miss you.

CONTENTS

ACKNOWLEDGMENTS

I fell in love with words as a child. When my father, Pryce, or brother, Ike, would knit them together through stories, they fell across my hungry soul and covered me with an afghan of comfort for many long hours at a time.

I didn't come out of the womb with the same panache for weaving my own stories, as my dad and brother did, so I longed to be a roving journalist who would uncover stories rather than create them. Somewhere along the squiggly lines of growing up, though, shame took root, and I didn't think I was good enough—or smart enough—to live my dream.

Then, God gave me a second chance. His life-giving breath blew me into the arms of a husband who saw the dream God had for me when I could not see it for myself. Through many years of blindness, Milton was my eyes. When the deafening drums of shame beat out the sound of my heart's music, Milton somehow heard over the clanging noise and sang my own song to me, until finally I began to keep the rhythm for myself.

This book would not be if it were not for Milton, my husband, lover, and best friend, because I would never have survived the stories of adventure and danger held within—and others this book could not contain—were it not for his love, forgiveness, and most of all, his balancing presence in my life. Thank you for not running away, even when I did.

Once I found the courage to write, the daunting process of finding a publisher began. Then, again, God's mighty breath blew just the right person along. Greg Johnson, aka Agent 007, agreed to represent my work, although the first pile I presented him closely resembled a shaken sack of Scrabble letters strewn across a game board.

Greg believed in the stories God gave me. He also knew I needed help to get past the blur of emotions that kept tangling up my many words. So, he sent me to a coach who not only taught me how to cull words, but also to trust my heart for the beauty it would pump onto the page. Ken Gire, thank you for teaching me to love, hone, and protect the stories God gives me more than my words, or ego.

Greg also led me to David C Cook, my publisher. The entire team—from editing to marketing—has shown such passion and compassion for this work that I never doubt it's the presence of Christ binding us together, not a contract. The greatest gift from that relationship is my editor Susan Tjaden who poised my passion with her dev-edit sixth sense, the instinct of exactly where to place each boxcar in my long train of story.

No woman ever really survives any sort of birthing without the sweat and support of other women. Mom, Bethany, Ida Mae, Whitney, Olivia, Audrey, Claudia, Louise, Lauran, Terry, Brooke, and Lindsey, thank you for being women who do your own unique form of dancing, crying, howling, loving, serving, being, and sharing that makes you so strong you're not afraid of the wild-unstoppable thing God does in and through me. I would not be the woman I am if you were not the beautiful women you are.

Lastly, and in the spirit of "the last shall be made first," I owe so much to one other. I would have never heard the stories, rode the donkey, kissed the lips of the dying, been washed in the mysterious blood of mother and child, born the pain, laughed in the moonlight, passed through the darkness, or found my way out if it were it not for the loyal man I am humbled to call my partner and friend, James Lual Atak.

> *Love, undying gratitude, and celebration for*
> *each of you and the lives you offer,*

k

Foreword

I first met Kimberly Smith when she visited our Eternal Perspective Ministries office. EPM had been supporting Make Way Partners, and Kimberly came to share more about their outreach to the orphans in Darfur, Sudan.

I was in the process of writing my book *If God Is Good*, so I interviewed Kimberly about the suffering she had witnessed and the light God was shining in the darkness. Later I met her husband, Milton, and thanked him for releasing his precious wife for the cause of Christ. At the time I wasn't aware of the trauma she had endured while in Darfur.

It's astounding that Kimberly and Make Way Partners were able to establish an orphanage in southern Sudan, one of the poorest nations in the world with one of the highest rates per capita of victims of human trafficking and enslavement. The challenges seemed insurmountable, and yet by God's grace, it happened. And now other orphanages are being built.

We've been privileged to continue our partnership with Kimberly in the ministry of Make Way Partners. I'm glad to see *Passport through Darkness*, as this is a remarkable story that needs to be told.

While reading this book, you may weep and ask, "Why?" It's not easy to think about traumatized and abused children. You may be tempted to stop reading. Kimberly's poignant story of the dire situations she dealt with will stay with you for a long time. But facing the distressing realities can move you into caring for the widows and orphans so close to God's heart: "Religion that is pure and undefiled before God, the Father, is this: to visit orphans and widows in their affliction" (James 1:27).

Kimberly shares her own journey honestly and from the heart. While serving these precious orphans, she suffered at the hands of those who didn't care about her or the work she was doing. But God in His faithfulness has given her strength and help to work through her trauma as she continues to serve the extremely needy children of this world. I commend her for telling her story to be of greater service to God's people.

I know Kimberly and Milton's desire is that what you read in this book will be used of God to motivate you to action on behalf of vulnerable children around the world. In the process, as you walk with Kimberly, you may also find perspective, forgiveness, and healing in your own life.

May God use His servant's story to His glory. Not only Kimberly's story, but yours and mine as well.

Randy Alcorn
Author of Heaven *and* If God Is Good

EVERYONE HAS OCEANS TO FLY, AS LONG AS
THEY HAVE THE HEART TO DO IT.
IS IT RECKLESS? MAYBE, BUT WHAT DO
DREAMS KNOW OF BOUNDARIES?

Amelia Earhart, from *Amelia*

ESPECIALLY THE ONES OUR CREATOR BREATHES
INTO THE CHAMBERS OF OUR HEARTS.

Kimberly L. Smith

Chapter 1

AT THE END OF ME

I stood at a precipice, a crag of rock in a parched, thirsty land that mirrored the condition of my heart. From where I stood, I looked down upon the riverbed that rendered the jagged cut reaching from the left corner of my mouth down to the bottom of my chin, and my right eye purplish black.

I recalled the day these marks came upon me and considered how many of the women I saw laboring in the current below who shared my experience. Fifty percent? Ninety percent? Had any woman been spared the hand-delivered scars of violence birthed in the tomb of this brutal, war-torn land?

Sickly cows wove around and between the women in the river. As the cows did their business in the water, some of the women bathed. Others washed rags they donned as clothing. Still others drew cans of drinking water from the soapy-feculent murkiness.

Taking stock of the last few months spent here at the border of Darfur, Sudan—the cusp of hell—I savored how God had knit these women into the fiber of my soul in ways that I'd never imagined possible back in the day of my corporate-ladder climbing. Love for them had changed my whole world. It had changed me. Now it was time for me to take what I'd been shown here back to my home in America with prayers that it, too, would be transformed.

My soul felt as restless and insecure as my feet did shuffling at the edge of the cliff.

A part of me felt so dark, lonely, and overwhelmed, I wanted to throw myself from the spire and be done with it. That would be the easy way, though, and my life had never seemed to be about finding the easy path. In fact, something in me seemed to like making life as difficult as possible.

A sprig of hope, a mite of faith encouraged me to stand down. Wait. Be expectant, but don't jump. Pray. Help was surely around the corner.

Voice of the Martyrs (VOM) had promised to send someone to witness the persecution, rape, mutilation, and genocide I was documenting on the southern border of Darfur. Knowing it had taken me months of preparation, followed by endless fieldwork, to find and accurately record this data—information that I was still just beginning to comprehend—I didn't see how I could possibly help the VOM rep grasp it in just three days.

Sudan is the tenth-largest country in the world; the region of Darfur is the size of France. The southern half of Sudan has a grand total of about three miles of pavement. Darfur has none. The reality of war, insecurity, violence, and lack of infrastructure, combined with the fact that we had no vehicle to speed up our maneuvers, rendered the task of sufficiently covering the vast territory in such a short time frame all but impossible.

I'd taken it upon myself to take the time and risk of walking from village to village or riding our sole motorbike to the death camps, what I'd come to call the Internally Displaced People's camps (IDP). I started calling IDPs death camps after my first visit over a year ago. Before that trip, the word *camp* always conjured an image of security, even if the conditions were rustic. Visiting one stripped me of my penchant for naiveté, showing me thousands of people squatting in the desert with no food, water, or security—just waiting for death. For most, the wait wasn't long.

I wanted to make sure I would be able to adequately expose the VOM rep to the same kind of reality. To do that, I would need transportation to cover vast amounts of ground more quickly than walking would allow.

Late yesterday a brainstorm hit me. We'd ride donkeys! James Lual Atak, our indigenous director, laughed at my *kawaidja* (rich white person) notions, calling me a Sudanese wannabe. But he humored me. Since the VOM rep would be here in just a few days, early this morning he'd brought several donkeys to our camp so we could test-ride them before the rep arrived.

Always ready for action, I was the first to climb on. An old man we called Peterdit held the end of the rope tied around the neck of my donkey, which I'd named Blue. The sharp ridge of spine rising from Blue's bare back cut into me in all the wrong places, and I squirmed to make a seat for myself.

Peterdit kept overenunciating two Arabic words for me, one for stop and one for faster. As Blue reared up, alternately kicking his hind legs and then his front legs high into the air, he let me know he wasn't happy about my squirming on his backside.

Blue's outburst jerked the rope from Peterdit's grasp. Blue set off toward the village, bucking like a horizontal kangaroo.

In my hysteria I could only summon up one of the two words Peterdit taught me. I screamed it as firmly as I could, *"Harach! Harach! Harach!"* over and over again trying to make Blue obey my limited grasp of the Arabic language: "Stop!"

My head thrashed back and forth, and I flopped to Blue's side, squeezing my legs around his girth as tightly as I could, while clinging to the frayed rope now burning the palms of my hands as it ripped through my fingers. As I blitzed by, I caught a glimpse of James laughing uproariously from atop his donkey, his long legs conveniently reaching his feet flat to the desert floor. At the time, I found no humor in Blue's fit, or my condition!

After my whirlwind tour of the village via Blue's conniption, Peterdit boldly stepped into Blue's path and grabbed the rope flinging freely in the air as I clung to Blue's short tuft of mane. He yelled a word I did not recognize in such force that the beast calmed himself, and I fell to the ground. Although my body would yell its trauma to me through deep musculature aches for many days, my only serious injury was to my pride.

Apparently the one Arabic word I had been yelling was not the word "Stop!" but rather "Faster, faster, faster!"

The comedy of my barebacked-donkey ride at this morning's sunrise seemed a millennium away, and a stark contrast to the bleakness of what followed. As waves of heat swelled from the desert floor, I wrote off the whole donkey deal as another one of my romantic inclinations, and James and I opted to walk, not ride, to the death camp.

While there may be few good days in a death camp, this one was particularly brutal. We'd been out of medicine for a month, out of food for a week, and today, we ran out of water. All of those life-giving commodities were gone, except for the private stash we kept at our compound for James and me, the kawaidja.

Although at home in the United States, people often thought of me as a poor missionary, I was coming to understand and grapple with the fact that I was, in reality, wealthy for simple things like never running out of water.

Up to this point in my life, what had I chosen to do with my riches? Standing on that cliff, I painfully acknowledged how I'd squandered so much of what God had given me, most painfully my entire life. Many times throughout this journey, this awakening, I have come perilously close to throwing it all away.

Through God's grace, I slowly stepped down from the precipice and began to face the end of the me I'd created for myself. I wanted to live the life—be the *me*—He dreamed of.

I remembered a prayer I'd cried out many years before, begging Him to use me. I wondered, if I'd known where that prayer would lead, would I still have prayed it? Deciding the answer was yes, I uttered a new prayer: "You can have whatever You want from me, but please, God, just show me what difference one person can make in the darkness of this broken world."

The following is His story, as lived through me to this point.

Chapter 2

THE ROAD TO A LIFE
THAT MATTERS

When our lives aren't what we long for them to be, we often fall into blaming someone else. At first glance all of our problems appear to be because we didn't get something—or someone—we wanted. It often takes years of life chipping away at us before we're willing to peek inside ourselves for the source of our discontent.

For me, the motivation to stop blaming others—and look inside myself—came at a great cost. My first husband and I labeled each other as the source of our own discontent. Tragically, after almost ten years of marriage, we divorced. Broken pieces of our family's heart were grounded into the street of despair like a shattered Coke bottle under the steamroller of anger, blame, and bitterness.

As I carefully examined the cesspool I'd made of my life back then, I spotted a stone God had carefully placed under my feet, keeping me safe and dry. Through His mercy and bountiful grace, He'd given me a second chance at a home, a marriage, and a family. A life.

Milton, my husband of more than twenty years now, is both ferocious in battle and gentle in ways of the heart that even few women embody. He is the perfect mate for me.

Both of us had emerged from failed marriages that mirrored our upbringing. So we entered our marriage together with gusto, coming at each other with fierce determination to weather the blur of life's mixer with eyes wide open.

We each threw our three children into the family blender, hoping to create something beautiful out of all the slicing and dicing. With five girls and one boy ranging from toddler to teens, there would be plenty of nosh to tempt us into closing our eyes—or worse—our hearts. At times, we fought for one another. At times, against. Other times, we squeezed our eyes shut in fear, anger, or pain—but never our hearts.

Soon I began to see God's stones everywhere. Having grown up on the wrong side of the tracks, I'd since worked hard to achieve the lifestyle I imagined to be on the other side. At the top of my game I became a successful executive in corporate America.

I had a good life. But it wasn't enough. Something essential was missing. Even with my feet dry and secure on those perfectly placed stones, a nagging sense of futility needled away at me day and night.

When I first became conscious of this emptiness, I thought maybe it was just because I was getting older, and all of the "big firsts" were behind me. I wasn't going to have any more children. I couldn't keep climbing the corporate ladder at the same pace forever; that high was gone. My marriage was good, but not the hot romance it was at first.

I dragged in from the office late most evenings, struggled to keep the kids on track, strove to keep the house in order, fought crow's-feet and cellulite, and scored check marks beside church attendance and Bible reading. Things looked pretty good … on the outside.

I thought living the "good life" would make my family happy and secure.

I was wrong. It wasn't working.

Something was missing. Even when nestled in my own bed in the arms of my loving husband in a house full of beautiful children, I often woke up in the middle of the night lonely, with a haunting feeling in my stomach. Pursuit of the American Dream was eating me alive.

Asleep at the Wheel of Life

By the late nineties, we were living near Birmingham, Alabama, and had two children left at home. Life was a lot less demanding, and I began to listen to that restless growl in my soul a bit more.

Early one Monday morning, before the fog had time to clear the basin between the twin peaks of Double Oak Mountain, I cut through the murkiness in my company-supplied Mercury Grand Marquis. As usual, I clipped off the miles of my forty-five-minute commute from our home in the country to my urban office by alternately talking on a cell phone and speaking notes for the day into my handheld recorder.

While I multitasked and watched for flashing taillights ahead and reflectors along the white lines at the edge of the foggy mountain road, images filled my mind as if a movie were playing in my head.

In this movie, I saw myself dressed in my typical business attire, sporting manicured nails and flawless makeup, talking away on my cell phone. It was just like any other workday commute—until I reached intersecting County Road 43. Rarely traveled by the public, County Road 43 was favored by large logging trucks. They could barrel through the twists and turns, confident no sheriff would catch them, or even care. County Road 43 had not yet caught the eye of developers as most of the county had, and the few shacks it hosted were filled with long-forgotten families of once-. upon-a-time sharecroppers. A tangle of overgrowth obscured the intersection.

The drama playing in my head suddenly intensified, with images so vivid I felt as though I were really living them:

> *A Mack truck barrels along County Road 43, unaware he is approaching a busy highway. The driver of the truck thinks he is tunneling through one more cluster of low hanging trees along a winding stretch of county road.*
>
> *He sees the bush, but he does not see the stop sign ensnarled within it. The truck runs the stop sign. I don't even see him coming. He plows right through me.*
>
> *The moment of impact. The deafening sound of crushing metal, twisting, grinding. Glass shattering. Pieces of both vehicles tumbling through the air, scraping across the road. And me, flying slow motion through the windshield, tumbling across the slick metal hood, then sprawling onto the dirt like a rag doll, bloodied and broken, coming to rest facedown and split asunder on the shoulder of the road.*

Startled by the scene as it unfolded in my mind, I broke into a cold sweat. Mercilessly, the movie played on:

> *Quick cut to our home in the country. Milton, still in his bathrobe, getting the kids ready for school. The phone ringing. Milton reaching for it, listening. An officer breaking the news to*

*him. His face going slack, growing pale. The news hitting him
like a punch. Pushing the receiver into his stomach, he curls
over, crying, "No. No. Kimberly. No."*

*He drops the receiver. The children run to the kitchen where
he is crying. Milton pushes out the best words he can find, "A
truck hit Mom. She's dead. Mom is gone."*

With tears streaming down my cheeks, images continued to
flicker through my mind as I kept driving:

*The office where I worked. My boss's phone ringing. Getting
the news, shaking his head. A tear sliding down his check.*

*Later that afternoon. My boss sending out a corporate
memo about my death. Everything stopping, for a day. Everyone
stunned, for a day.*

*The day before the funeral, the local paper posts my obitu-
ary. My life reduced to three column inches of type, along with
a photograph. A younger, more flattering picture, followed by
a thumbnail sketch of my accomplishments, and a list of who
survived me.*

*The day of the funeral, my boss gives my staff the day off
so they can attend.*

*The day after my funeral, human resources places an ad
to fill my position in the same newspaper that—just a few
days earlier—announced my tragic death.*

That was it.

Life went on.

At least for everyone else.

I had worked hard for what I thought was the right thing for me, and for my family. Now, I was dead. And with my death, everything in which I had invested the majority of my time was gone too. It left no lasting value of any kind.

Death revealed my life to be a well-concealed Ponzi scheme. A swindle. A farce. A compromise. I had fooled everyone.

Even myself.

Wide Awake

Shaken by this unsettling vision, I considered my children. They were great kids and good students, but kids whose main concerns were to be popular athletes, pretty cheerleaders, or to drive cool cars. They were excellent students of every stride I'd made chasing the American Dream—collecting things, pursuing achievements, and looking great on the outside. All of this at the expense of what their hearts most deeply longed for—to know the exact reason God created them and how to spend their entire lives from that sacred place. It hurt to realize the values I handed down to them.

Even in our church we didn't teach our kids about being a part of something bigger. We tried mostly to make sure we provided enough entertainment in their religion to hook them into our church so we didn't lose them to the competition. Sometimes we feared the competition would be a boyfriend, other times a drug pusher, still other times another church.

Sure, we did soup kitchens and extracurricular goodness, but these activities were tack-ons, not a way of life.

To be honest, we adults in the church weren't a whole lot different. We, too, seemed to prefer "fun" over transformation—only our definition of fun was just a little more refined. Over time, it had been diluted to something more like comfort.

In a heartbeat, I knew: *This is the emptiness that wakes me in the middle of the night, the ravenous hunger inside me that howls and growls but nothing seems to fill.*

I longed to know that not just what I *did* mattered, but that *I* mattered—my *life* mattered. I longed to feel God's pleasure as when He first delighted in Adam and Eve, saying, "It is very good."

I couldn't imagine God looking at my life and saying, "It is very good." At best He might say something like, "Well, at least she's trying to check off the right things. It's just too bad she doesn't see how I made her to shine, brighten the world, and live free."

That's when it hit me.

Nothing could fill the emptiness.

Not work, no matter how many promotions I achieved. Not money, no matter how much I earned. Not family, no matter how proud they made me. Not power, no matter how much I acquired. Not vacations, no matter how exotic they were.

The "movie" I experienced on my early-morning commute looped through my head so many times that I gave it a title: *The Mack Truck Syndrome.* Unfortunately, Angelina Jolie wasn't the star; I was. And I was dying inside. I found myself stuck in a meaningless plot that was going nowhere, moving through empty scenes that made no sense, reading lines that fell flat.

Can you blame me for wanting to walk off the set?

I longed to make a bold move with my life. Yet I had no clue where to begin. Or how. With each passing day I grew more desperate. Nights were the worst. Awake and crying my way through most of them, I had only one prayer: "God, use me or take me out. Please, I am begging You. I don't want to live this way. I can't live this way any longer. I'm desperate to know why I'm here. Use me or take me out."

Although I was blind to it at first, over time—painstaking time—doors began to open. One tentative step at a time, through that prayer of desperation, I inched my toe across the threshold into a new way of living and began the journey of finding the life where I would discover the exact reason He created me and know His delight in me.

Chapter 3

FROM DARKNESS
TO THE DAWN

At the same time the *The Mack Truck Syndrome* awakened me to my God-size hole of emptiness, something was shifting in Milton. He began talking differently and musing about wanting to get outside the life box into which his days neatly folded.

He began saying things like, "Let's do something meaningful, something that makes a difference in people's lives. In our lives."

He complained, "My life has morphed into making a living instead of living my life. I want more adventure. I want to know my life matters, even if it means taking great risks."

It was enough for me that I was coming unplugged and wanting out of whatever security corporate America offered. I wasn't sure I liked Milton having similar thoughts. Fear threatened to cripple my journey before I ever really took off.

It was one of those times in life when I wanted to have my cake and eat it too. I wanted to feel the deep joy God promises when we completely surrender to Him, but I also wanted to have all the things I'd come to rely on, like a brimming bank account. I stood at a crossroad like that from my mental movie on County Road 43. I feared stepping out and being hit by the Mack truck, but I knew life's traffic doesn't stop and I'd better decide which direction I was headed. Couldn't Milton pull over to the shoulder of life's road for a while, stay focused on realities like bill paying and child rearing while I calculated the risk of jumping lanes?

Day by day I watched Milton hold the span of tension between his responsibilities and the stirrings of his heart. On the one hand, I wanted him to lead us down this unknown path; on the other hand, I was afraid to follow. I knew enough to know once we took the first step toward finding God's heart—His plan for us at that moment in our shared history—my illusions of control would be stripped away.

Milton kept saying, "It's not either/or, Kimberly. There's a way to live both responsibly and passionately. Just because we're taught to 'find a job, make a living, buy a house, create a family, and amass retirement funds' doesn't mean we have to follow that model. Maybe God wants something more out of our lives."

I kept hearing, "We're going to do something crazy. We're not going to be able to raise our kids the way I want. We're going to look ridiculous." His words bumped into my past of being poor, my drive to achieve wealth, and what I thought was security.

Milton was driven. He was intent on finding a way to live from his heart and be responsible. He read books. He explored men's groups. He met with fellow clergy. I became an ostrich burying my head, hoping I wouldn't have to engage him in this struggle.

A Chance Encounter

Then, as if by chance, Milton went downtown for a meeting. While in the waiting room, he restlessly thumbed through a magazine and stumbled upon an article calling for missionaries to serve in Spain.

In the early 1980s, Milton had been a missionary in Spain. He'd gone shortly after dictator Francisco Franco died. Under Franco's oppression, Spain had been more like Africa than Europe. Milton had the time of his life learning a new language, navigating a foreign culture, and exploring new ways of preaching in a closed society.

Instinctively, before he even finished reading the article, Milton knew that was the life he missed. It was the life he longed for and wanted to give his family.

He came home naively thinking his passion would be contagious. He laid out what felt to me a solid plan for self-destruction. He was so clear. So certain.

Milton's passion for this radical change threw me off kilter. I was horrified. It threatened everything I clung to, especially my illusions of security and control provided by my career and money. Yes, I wanted to find God's pleasure. Yes, I wanted to know my purpose, but the price of selling our beautiful home in the country, ditching furniture and everything we owned just seemed too extreme. For two months I reasoned, "Surely we can find a compromise."

For two months—while I pouted—Milton moved ahead, made phone calls, explored possibilities, and blueprinted a new life. Anger seeded in me, threatening to blossom into full-bloom resentment. I tried to create a stalemate that would slow him down, but the man was on a mission, and he was invincible to my attempts to distract him with fear.

Negotiations

Early one morning, at the peak of my stonewalling, I sat alone in our kitchen peering out a window into the darkness. I tried to pray but instead found myself comparing the black predawn to the condition of my heart.

As the sun rose and glistened on a neighbor's dewy horse farm, it brought light to everything I feared losing. I felt pressed to choose between all the things around me—which seemed to constitute my daily life—and my marriage. It was no choice at all.

Milton wasn't pushing me, much less threatening our marriage, yet he was moving into uncharted territory without me. I wanted to be on the back of that wild horse with him, but that required trusting Milton with the reins. It also meant facing my fear that I might fail, be a klutz, fall off and break my neck, or something even worse. Still, I knew something would be forever lost if I didn't listen to his crazy heart, meet him in this struggle, and saddle up.

While the sun dried the morning's last dew, I finally reached out in a desperate prayer for a scrap of direction. Any scrap. As I cried out, I heard myself speak the word "Compromise."

It hit me hard.

As I prayed, I realized I treated God as if He were my spotter, and I—the beginner gymnast—had grown as far as I could because I wouldn't risk the next level since I didn't trust my spotter. I feared He would drop me.

I'd cried, "Use me or take me out," but I wanted to be used on *my* terms, with security and a prerevealed outcome.

I wanted to find my purpose and feel His pleasure, but I wanted certain guarantees. I wanted a plan to follow that assured success. I wanted checks and balances in my bank account, and I wanted a backup plan in case God didn't come through. I had a foot in both worlds, and the breach threatened to tear me apart.

I've always been hailed as a great negotiator. It hit me hard to realize that I had been asking not only Milton, but also God, for a compromise—a safety net should they both fail me.

Free-falling

Filled with fear, but desperate for a taste of the life I had only
dreamed of, I prayed for the courage to let go of the many things
that insulated me from my hunger—my passion. I longed to climb
on that wild stallion my husband rode so fearlessly.

As I broke down, sliding off the stool on which I sat and spilling
onto the floor, God met me in my place of despair. Another dry
stone gently placed beneath my feet …

As I wept, I felt His arms envelop me. He gave me images of
Milton riding like the wind, carried by a great stallion. God. God
carried Milton, and I could climb on and ride too, if only I chose.

In the images of my mind, I did choose. I jumped on, wrapped
my arms around Milton's chest, and clamped my legs around as
much of the girth of our Great Stallion as they could reach. I was on.
I wasn't letting go no matter where the journey took us. Milton's face
beamed with pride, knowing I covered his back. My hair flew behind
me as we took charge for an unknown destination.

By the time Milton roused for his first cup of coffee, I was ready
to face him for the first time in two months. No more feigned moue.
No more holding back. No more trying to seduce him into a life of
comfort.

Milton has lived with me so long and well that he feels my
rhythms. He senses my energy and knows my spirit. The moment
he walked into the kitchen, he knew I was with him on the journey.

He cried as I relayed my dawning from the dark pit, and
together, we began to pray our way through the steps we would take
to walk into the unknown life that stretched ahead of us. Together,
we became watchmen for the dry stones in troubled waters.

Chapter 4

WE'RE NOT IN
KANSAS ANYMORE

The next twelve months proved to be every bit the adventure my horse-riding metaphor promised. We were accepted by a mission agency, sold our home and cars, gave away or sold our furniture, raised funds, home-schooled our only two girls still in the nest (Whitney, thirteen, and Olivia, eleven), sat long into many nights laughing and crying our way through bittersweet good-byes with friends and family we would leave behind ... and moved to Spain.

For the first time in my life, I lived in the center of a loud and lusty city, Salamanca, near the border of Portugal. Of course, we didn't have air-conditioning, but—with bars closing about the time I normally awakened—trying to sleep with our windows open was about as fruitful as lying down to take a nap on Bourbon Street during Mardi Gras.

In contrast to the bustling nights, daytime in Spanish culture moved slowly. It took an entire day to accomplish even the simplest of tasks.

During the first six months, at least one of our daughters, Whitney or Olivia, would come home from their Spanish-speaking school every day crying, "Mama, I can't even understand if I'm in history or biology class."

Our family motto became "We're not in Kansas anymore, Toto."

Around the six-month mark, some of the foreignness began to

wane, and we found a certain rhythm. By our first anniversary, both girls spoke Spanish like natives and passed all their subjects.

I discovered how to make fun out of the monotonous daily runs required of me by learning to rollerblade. I rollerbladed to the meat market, produce stand, bread shop, egg farm, and practically everywhere I went. The Spaniards laughed at me, but it was a great conversation starter. Finally, we settled into our new lives and made a home for ourselves.

Ministry Beginnings

Milton and I were codirectors of a student ministry at the University of Salamanca. Students came from Japan, Germany, France, Korea, and literally all over the world in order to study the pure Castilian Spanish. In any given week we hosted students from upward of twenty-five countries in our tiny inner-city apartment.

Many of these students had never even heard the name Jesus. For many of them, it was their first time away from home. They were often lonely, looking for a way to connect, and wide open to the gospel.

Spain is a party country, though. Regular fiestas meant our students were often out of school—sightseeing Europe—and leaving Milton and me with free time on our hands.

We started a street ministry with our spare time, hoping some of the students would get involved with it too. A British couple heard about what we were doing and told us of a home across the border in Portugal that they believed housed African immigrant children. The Brits told us the couple running the home was desperate for help. We decided to go check it out for ourselves.

An Introduction to the Dark Side of Ministry

Portugal is a member of the European Union. It has regulations for the care of children, regardless of their race, ethnicity, or citizenship. However, we couldn't believe our eyes when we walked into the home: The nineteen children in this shanty were sleeping in dank rooms with holes in the plywood roof so large I could literally stick my head through the ceiling.

When it rained, buckets of water soaked their beds. It was January and the temperature hovered just above freezing. There was no heat for the children. All of them bellowed deep coughs.

Quarter-size droplets of condensation clung to the kitchen ceiling from where they slowly dripped like small clear suction cups losing their grip and splashing onto the long narrow plank of a table. When the children gathered at sunrise, they were given tea for breakfast. For lunch, they ate a piece of white bread with water and thin soup for dinner.

Buster, the man running the home, asked Milton and me for money. We couldn't make sense of the circumstances. Something seemed terribly out of sorts with the whole situation.

We probed. We wanted to know why the home didn't receive help from the Portuguese government. Buster explained that he and his wife were Christians and wanted to teach the children about Jesus. He said if they accepted government funding, then "Jesus talk" would not be allowed.

It was true—all of the children could quote the Bible like tape recorders. Still, something resonated seriously wrong.

Milton and I decided against giving the couple cash. However, we bought food, medicine, clothes, and building supplies to repair the home where the children slept.

When friends and supporters heard what we were doing, many came to help. Students from Japan and England who had studied with us in Spain joined us. An entire family came from Germany, as well as many Americans.

Save an Orphan's Life, or Protect Our Own Children?

During this time, we were able to get closer to the orphans. One day, Carlos, a little boy of only nine years, came to me.

"Auntie Kimberly. Auntie Kimberly! Where is the Vaseline?"

I was busy preparing lunch for the team and offhandedly told him, "Carlos, I don't know where the Vaseline is. Go ask someone else."

"I can't ask anyone else. Uncle Buster told me I can't talk to anyone about the Vaseline."

That got my attention. I stopped my activities and knelt down, eye-level to the small boy before me. "Well, Carlos, I still don't know where the Vaseline is, but I will help you find it. By the way, though, why do you need the Vaseline?"

With my question, Carlos grew very anxious and began bouncing from foot to foot. "My bum is bleeding."

(*Bum* is a British slang word for buttocks.)

"Oh my gosh, Carlos! Why is your bum bleeding?"

More anxious, Carlos showed me his backside. The child was cut, torn, and bloody. His flesh bore signs of trauma, old and new.

I ran to Milton. Milton immediately went to the authorities. I stayed at the home trying to pretend everything was okay in hopes Uncle Buster didn't grow suspicious. The first day, the authorities turned Milton away. He fought all day, but no one would help.

Both child-welfare services and the police department told him, "Those kids aren't even Portuguese citizens; there is nothing we can do."

Hoping my firsthand testimony would help, the next day I went with Milton. This time, they kicked both of us out.

We kept going back, insisting someone talk with us. We snooped around to learn who was in charge of each phase of investigations. Each time we returned, we asked for a higher-ranking official, by name.

Eventually a social worker confided she wanted to help, but a higher-up had blocked her. Neither Milton nor I knew what to do. We were in over our heads. I called the International Justice Mission; they were a huge encouragement. They told us, "Just don't leave. The authorities must know you will tell the world what is going on if they don't take appropriate action."

Milton and I became the ugly Americans in a whole new way. We did everything missionaries should never do. We flashed our blue passports. We made threats—which we full-well intended to see through. We threw as much weight around as a Sumo wrestler vying for a title. Our prize: freedom from sexual slavery for nineteen African children.

Finally, after many days of battles, denials, confrontations, and threats, the head of child-welfare services agreed to collect Carlos and take him to the hospital to be medically examined. His sodomy was confirmed, and the doctors admitted him into the hospital. Then the authorities stepped in and placed him in protective custody.

Rosita, a woman who worked in the home, told us she had been praying for a long time that someone would find out—and care—about what was happening to the children. She knew all of them, both boys and girls, were being forced into sexual activity. She had gone to the police, a judge, child-welfare services, and her church. No one listened to her. The hardest blow came from her pastor. He told her, as a woman, she should not speak badly about a man in the community.

Through Rosita, we learned a naive missionary couple had given Uncle Buster a surveillance camera, which Uncle Buster told them he needed for security. Instead of protecting the children, Uncle Buster used the camera to film the children in sexual activity and then posted it on the Internet.

Carlos was safe, but Rosita lost her job after his rescue and there were eighteen other children in that same home with no one left to monitor their welfare. The battle had to continue. We had no physical evidence on the remaining children, and Uncle Buster clamped down, sealing the door like stones at Pharaoh's tomb.

We made it clear to both the perpetrators and the authorities that we would not turn our backs on the children. We made thunderous noise and told everyone, including the media, what was going on. We would not stop until the children were safe, regardless of the cost.

By this time Uncle Buster was so furious, he threatened to kill us. When that didn't work, he threatened to take our daughters.

It was an unbearable predicament. We could see only two options. Option one was to save our own children and abandon these helpless orphans. Option two was to fight to save the orphans and thereby knowingly risk the lives and well-being of our own children. Again, an impossible choice.

Together, Milton and I dug deep into the parental potholes of right, wrong, life lessons, responsibility, protection, and nurture. After days of torment and still finding no answers in those pits, we climbed out—laying our fears and all possible outcomes at the feet of the One who fathers us all.

In all our parental angst we couldn't see what God would have us do. Falling on Him as not only our Father, but also the Father of our daughters—and the orphans—we saw that He cherished us all with no regard for our status, nationality, or familial lines. He didn't distinguish between "our children" and "the orphans." He'd placed these particular children under our care as surely as He had Whitney and Olivia. The Father of us all wasn't asking us to choose to protect one over the other, but—if we were to see *how* we could be faithful to His guidance—we'd have to be stretched to let go of much of our cultural expectations, especially regarding what responsible parenting looked like.

God used Whitney and Olivia as much as He did Milton and me.

After months of working with the orphans, both of the girls had fallen in love with them; their lives had grown forever intertwined. I had watched love filter through our girls and splash on the orphans as purely as water flows through a sieve.

Whitney and Olivia pleaded with us not to abandon the orphans, whom most considered throwaways. While I clung to my motherly conditioning and floundered in my commitment to the orphans, my beautiful teenage daughters begged me to do whatever it took to rescue the orphans.

Looking at our daughters' faces, hearing their cries, Milton once again took the lead. We knew our children would never respect us again if we walked away, even if we were walking away to protect them.

By this time Whitney was seventeen and Olivia fifteen. Unlike the orphans locked in the brothel with no one to fight for them, both our girls had a network of loving friends and family who would receive them. They would be safe in the United States while Milton and I fought for the orphans.

Together, Though Separated by Thousands of Miles

Even though we had talked, prayed, lamented, and looked for a way out, in the end we all agreed as a family what we needed to do. Certain, passionate, and teary-eyed, Milton and I sent Whitney and Olivia to stay with friends in Alabama. Milton and I remained in Portugal to press charges and insist the authorities investigate the home.

Even though roughly five thousand miles separated us, on some level our entire family fought to free the children still enslaved in their living hell. And, although it was something we all felt passionately committed to doing, it bore a cost. Ultimately, however, we'd be drawn tighter together as a family.

Our lives didn't look like any of the families our girls encountered back home. The horrors Whitney and Olivia had seen and heard, and the brokenness in our world with which they'd become so personally acquainted, made it impossible for them to blend in with other teenagers. Their sheer differentness isolated them socially, and depression weighed down on them.

Although we made many of these decisions as a family, we all suffered individual degrees of discouragement and angst. I often questioned myself, Milton, and even God's sanity throughout the battle.

On the darkest days, we often felt as if our whole family had free-fallen into an abyss. A few friends tried to encourage us; but even they had a hard time understanding why we would go to such an extreme to turn our lives upside down. They did not comprehend the evil we confronted—or what was at stake—so they often tried to encourage us to not "give so much" or "work so hard." Having looked Carlos straight in the eyes in the plight of his despair, we couldn't turn away any more than if he'd been our own child.

Still, our friends tried to help, and that brought comfort. Others often thought the whole topic of children being raped was too upsetting to even talk about, much less devote a ministry to. When I felt tempted to fall into self-pity, all I had to do was look at the faces of my beautiful daughters. Then I'd recall the sight of Carlos's backside bearing bloody scars of abuse. Instantly I'd be reminded that if I was taken out of commission, I'd pray night and day God would send someone to protect my daughters from the same fate Carlos had lived. *I* was that someone God had sent. *We* were the someones God had sent.

Once the investigation finally began in earnest, Milton and I were able to return to the States to be reunited with the girls and to begin the long process of healing the pain and loss marking our family.

As for the eighteen children who were still in the home after we rescued Carlos, it took two years of constant fighting to win their freedom. However, it was a bittersweet victory. Uncle Buster and his wife fled to Africa, where we fear they're working trafficking from the point of origin, in what are commonly referred to as source countries.

Ultimately, the children were sent back to the splintered family units that had turned them over to the malevolent couple in the first place. The Portuguese government withheld information as to how or where we could visit the children, write to them, or any way in which to follow up on their well-being.

Many times Milton and I filled to the brim with doubt. Feeling half-crazed, we questioned and retraced every step we took along the brambled path that led us to this insufficient second-place ending.

We felt no satisfaction in the shallow victory. Justice became something we understood to not exist in this world—especially for orphans who had no one to protect them.

The whole experience shook our very core and made personal for us why God would spend so much time talking through His Word about looking out for the orphans and widows. We knew their abuse and oppression broke His heart.

He'd taught us to pray "Thy Kingdom come, Thy will be done." Milton and I first began to seriously pray that prayer as a way to comfort ourselves when we felt most impotent in the battle against evil. On some level, praying "Thy Kingdom come, Thy will be done" haunted us, though. Gradually we began to understand that God didn't give us that prayer so much to comfort us as to mold and transform our hearts and lives.

The more we prayed "Thy Kingdom come …" the more it convicted us that God chose to use mankind—His incarnational presence in this world—to usher His Kingdom in, one fractured attempt at a time.

But who of us wants to give up our notion of what we think our lives should look like so that we are available for Him to use?

With each passing day we felt more rooted in the belief that when we prayed "Thy Kingdom come, Thy will be done" we were agreeing with God to give up our way of living to become the flesh and blood through which He grew His Kingdom.

This Kingdom living is painstaking work. We live it at times halfheartedly, other times with gusto, often with great joy and awe at the thrill of being used in something, anything, so far beyond ourselves we know it's God-sized. Almost always a dreadful fear hovers around, wanting to bear down on us, and more than a sprig of doubt pushes up like weeds through a sidewalk. Our only prayer in those times is "Lord, we believe. Help us in our unbelief!"

Partners against the Filth of Human Trafficking

Milton and I spent the two years we worked on the Portugal case to learn all we could about human trafficking—something I had never even heard of before this experience in the mission field. Where did the victims come from? Where were they sent? What kinds of things were they used for? Who was most vulnerable? How did the traffickers get them? Who ran the trafficking rings? Who profited by modern-day slavery, and where did the money go?

One of the surprising things we learned was that while sexual slavery is most commonly associated with Southeast Asia, it is actually growing faster in Eastern Europe and Africa than anywhere else in the world. This is mostly because of the swelling population of orphans and street children, the "throwaways."

Since many of the countries that are most vulnerable to

trafficking also experience high levels of Christian persecution, we developed a strategic partnership with Voice of the Martyrs. It was through a friendship with VOM's Eastern European and Northern African regional director, a Czech man named PJ, that we gained firsthand knowledge of trafficking in Eastern Europe.

Once we identified Transnistria, Moldova, and Bucharest, Romania, as the places where women and children were most vulnerable, PJ helped us to gain access and make contacts with indigenous Christian workers.

By this time, Milton and I knew we'd have to develop some sort of structure through which to answer the burden God placed on our hearts. We cofounded Make Way Partners to do just that.

Facing More Fear

Milton is an insulin-dependent diabetic. The travel and stress of fighting corruption took its toll on his organs, and eventually we based ourselves in the States for his medical care. Milton carved a niche for himself in research, training others, and mission development from the United States, while I began to do the international work alone.

PJ told me, "You know, Kimberly, what you are doing in Eastern Europe is very good. But, if you really want to do something about slavery, you'll go to Sudan. It's the worst place on the planet for this evil."

I didn't even consider PJ's request. I tried to put him off. Again, I stonewalled. I'd never dreamed of Africa. I'd never had a desire to go there. I made excuses, but the truth was that I was terrified of going to a place where mass rape, sexual slavery, persecution, and genocide were part and parcel of the daily routine.

But PJ was persistent. I figured my safest out was to tell him I'd talk to Milton about it. I was certain that my traditional, protective husband would never allow me to go to such a place without him.

I should have known that by the time I went to Milton, he had already been praying about it. He was painfully honest with me about his spiritual journey as he saw me stepping more and more to the front lines of where God led Make Way Partners, while his health kept pushing him to the background.

Tension between what Milton wanted, what he felt God wanted, and what he was concerned I'd end up doing—with or without his blessing—furrowed deep lines across his forehead. I could almost taste his anguish.

He wanted to keep his wife safe and by his side. He also wanted to be obedient and keep his eye on eternity, not just the here and now. He knew of the horrors against God and mankind taking place in Sudan and felt God wanted Make Way Partners in that battle. He could not go. I could. Again, the impossible choice.

Milton knew something about me that I could not yet admit. He knew that while I admitted I was afraid, in the end I'd never let fear keep me from doing something I thought I should do. If anything, it challenged me to go for it. Milton knew that even though I was afraid, the more I read about the horrors the women and children in Sudan suffered, the more I would grow determined to go.

At the time, I was only conscious of fear for my safety and compassion for the children's suffering. This fear and compassion fueled a fire of angst compelling me to take some kind of action—to take flight or fight. I had this fear of wimping out and was always afraid I'd fail or run from the fight. Milton knew me better than I knew myself.

Locking eyes and squeezing my hands, Milton told me, "I knew this day was coming. I ache. I'm afraid of losing you. If I lose you, I lose more than a piece of me; I lose who I've grown into being. And yet, something so strong within me knows you need to go. I can't even believe I'm saying this; but … I choose to let you go."

Not exactly the outcome I expected. I lost my easy out.

PJ kept calling.

I realized Milton was just as afraid as I was, and somehow that gave me courage because his example of leaning on God was so clear. It was so outside of his nature to release me in this way, especially since I didn't plead, bargain, or even seriously ask. I only posed the possibility.

Surrender didn't answer all of our questions, but it gave us both the peace to take baby steps toward obedience.

As Milton and I prayed throughout 2004 about my going to Sudan, the Darfur conflict exploded. Hundreds of thousands were murdered by their genocidal president. He also commissioned rape, sexual slavery, and plunder as spoils for the soldiers and militia who did his bidding.

I held my breath in a mixture of fear and excitement, barely able to believe it when I finally answered PJ's call and heard myself say, "Okay. So when are we going to Sudan?"

Chapter 5

AT THE RIVER'S EDGE

Since my submissive-wife facade had been blown to kingdom come, I agreed to go to Sudan to identify indigenous Christian leaders whom God was already using to protect women and children from slavery and other ravages of war.

If I could find such people, Make Way Partners would supply support, funds, and additional resources for these indigenous ministries. I figured one trip would do it, and I'd never have to return to Sudan. That was my plan anyway.

That first visit to Sudan was a miserable short-term mission trip. My Czech friend was not the one in charge of logistics, and it was so poorly planned that much of our time was wasted trying to get last-minute charters into the war-torn, restricted-access country.

Poor communication compounded logistical problems. I was not told, for example, I would be the only female of the twenty-plus member team until I met up with the men in Nairobi, Kenya.

While waiting in Nairobi for our disorganized leader to get us into Sudan, I could think of only two things. One, since I knew there were no toilets or outhouses in Sudan, I wondered who would cover my back as I squatted in the desert to relieve myself.

And two, I feared what would happen if we encountered the Janjaweed, the Muslim militia executing the rape, slavery, and genocide plaguing the country. Since Milton's health kept him from traveling with me, and since I didn't know these men I traveled with,

I feared if we were attacked, they just might give me over to the Janjaweed in order to save their own hides.

Once in Sudan, my frustrations and fears faded into the background as I faced others' suffering on a scale I'd never even imagined.

As I walked the fields in the Shilluk Kingdom of South Sudan, picking up tiny, singed, and mismatched flip-flops from the dirt floors of burned-down *tukels* (round, thatched-roofed mud huts of the Sudanese), echoes of crying children, long gone, haunted me.

Broken pots, strewn from one end of the field to the other, lay next to AK-47 bullet casings or in the trenches of military tank tracks. Human and animal remains and feces littered the ground. Walking the fields, I wondered how many diseases I literally stepped into.

Choosing My Tribe

One afternoon the tribal leaders called a meeting with us, the kawaidjas. Our group clumped together on the ground facing theirs. Men from both sides began talking about the five decades of Islamic invasion and what could be done to stop the senseless annihilation of an entire people.

I noticed no women attended the meeting. I spied them sitting off to the side of the field. I quietly left one sort of my tribe, the kawaidjas, for another—the women. We sat together in solidarity.

What I remember most is the way these gaunt women held themselves. They sat erect, holding their heads high with grace and dignity. Their gnarled and calloused bare feet bore witness to the thousands of barefoot miles they'd walked. The faded, tattered cloth wrapped around their emaciated bodies was incongruent with the bright, indestructible spirit radiating from within them.

At first I felt uneasy looking into their expectant eyes. What did I possibly have to offer these regal women? I wasn't famous or influential in any way. As I sat among them, my heart sank. I wanted to run away, forget I had ever seen those deep, hopeful eyes or those dark, expectant faces. Faces that were turned toward me. Eyes that were fixed on me. Waiting for *me* to say something, do something. Their Great White Hope sat there withering like an Easter lily too long in the glare of the African sun.

One woman's face, in particular, drew me. Dehydration, malnutrition, and constant exposure to the blistering sun sucked all moisture from her skin. So, while she was blacker than I'd ever seen human skin, her face still bore a chalky appearance.

I studied her face, body, hands, and feet for clues to her age. I considered asking her, but the war made that pointless since no records were kept. She would either tell me she didn't know, or she would make up an age. I figured she was younger than my forty-something years, but life had not been as kind to her.

Feeling pleasure from my attention, her black eyes softened in their yellow casings. Her lips curled up slightly in a shy smile, causing the skin on her neck to grow taut. That is when I saw them. Bite marks. Unmistakably human. Indescribably human. Unbelievably human. They had punctured both sides of her neck, still slightly open and enflamed. The wounds would leave permanent scars, I thought as I stared.

Seeing what she felt was revulsion in my eyes, she looked away. Her momentary pleasure from my attention quickly turned to shame. She tugged at the dirty rag she used for a scarf, pulling it over her head and wrapping it around her neck.

She dropped her head and scooted outside our circle. An older woman, missing most of her teeth, closed the circle by assuming her friend's position and spoke without prodding.

"I am Rebekah. She is Mary. Malakal is where the SPLA [Sudanese People's Liberation Army—the name for the South Sudan army opposing the Janjaweed] have their barracks. The North Sudan soldiers hate us because we live so close to the SPLA. They tell us if we are not Muslim, then we must be on the side of the SPLA, so they will kill us."

While Rebekah spoke, most of the other women sat in the dirt with their shriveled calves folded under their emaciated thighs, nodding in agreement or clucking their tongues against the roofs of their mouths in encouragement. A few stared off into some distant place in their minds, known only to themselves.

"Some time ago, soldiers came with the Janjaweed. I was asleep on my mat inside my tukel with my little baby suckling at my breast. I only had one sleeping mat so my older baby slept at my feet. He was two rainy seasons old. My daughter could not fit on the mat with us. She slept close to the cooking fire because it was her responsibility to make certain that the coal did not grow cold, or we would have no cooking fire the next day.

"Thunder crashed around us. It sounded far away, in the next village. I lay on my mat, thinking the rains were coming early this year. It clapped many times, over and over again, and drew closer. Then, a heavy thud. It sounded like a body dropping from the sky to the ground. It was quiet for just a moment, but then the explosion told me this was not thunder.

"Huge shells from the big tanks exploded all around us. I curled tighter around my baby at my breast to shield him from the bombs. Then the big trucks with guns mounted on top of them rolled between our tukels and fired right through them. I sat up, tying my baby to my breast so we could run away. I yelled for my daughter to grab my two-rainy-seasons-old son. I stuffed some maize in a cloth to tie around my waist as we ran. I knew we would not have a home to return to, and we would need food for our long journey to nowhere.

"I turned to my daughter when she screamed. She was holding my two-rainy-seasons-old son in her lap as blood ran from his little head. A bullet took him. We left him dead on my sleeping mat.

"Running outside my tukel, I saw the grass roof on fire. I looked up and down the village; I could see many, many tukels, and they all wore great fires on their roofs. My eyes first burned with tears for my son, but then they also burned from the smoke.

"The whole village ran toward the river Nile—just over there." Rebekah pointed her bony finger to the river.

"So, I ran toward the river too. I thought it was a good idea because if we had to hide for a long time, at least we could collect food from the river to eat. As we drew close to the Nile, gunships came roaring down the river at us. We turned to rush back into the bush, but they kept shooting anyway. Oh, they killed so many of us on that day.

"Some of us made it to the bush. We laid low on our bellies in the tall grass. When the night came, I pulled my baby from my back. Then I understood why he had not been crying to eat. A bullet found him on my back while I was running from the river's gunfire. I could not bury my baby. I could not keep him with me. The hyenas would come for us both. What could I do?

"I took the cloth from my back. I made it into a tiny bed for my baby. I folded it over many times to make his bed very soft. I took the wrap from my head to cover him. I left my baby in the bush. He was not alone. The hyenas would find him soon.

"We crawled low for many days, hiding in the bush. We were afraid to talk because the soldiers were hacking through the bush looking for us. We had no food. No water. Many more of us died from hunger and thirst in the bush than from the guns.

"When the soldiers found our men, they beat them or shot them straight away. But when they found us—the women—many of them would rape us over and over again.

"This is what happened to Mary. Many men raped her. So they marked her on both sides. She will not tell about it. None of our men will ever want her now.

"The Janjaweed rape our women. When they have spent them-selves on us, sometimes they continue to rape us with sticks. They tear out our womanhood so we can make no more Christian babies. They kill our men. What men remain will not take us as their wives because we are marked."

Rebekah lost her husband, her young child, and her baby, yet she sat with such composure and dignity recounting this madness. I had to know, and so I asked, "What about your daughter?"

Rebekah moved her long, lanky arm down the full length of her scrawny leg, reaching for the green rubber sandal in which her calloused foot rested. She fingered a hole at the heel.

Sadness pulled on Rebekah's face, the weight of it causing her shoulders to droop and her body to sag.

Still working the hole in her sandal, eyes downcast like a wounded child, Rebekah whispered, "My daughter did not have sandals."

"What happened to her?" I pushed.

"The soldiers. They took her."

I knew "took" meant raped. So I pressed on, "Where is she now?"

Her finger stopped its rotation around the perfectly formed hole in the heel of her green rubber sandal.

"I couldn't get to her. I had to save at least my baby. If I had gone to help her, I would have lost them both. So I hid in the bush—over there." Her long, slender finger languished toward the east edge of the field.

"I watched while soldier after soldier raped my little girl at the river's edge. When one finished, he would fire his gun into the air, howling with laughter while the next soldier jumped on her.

"When they finished with her, she lay so still I thought she was dead. One soldier wanted to keep her. He grabbed her dress and started dragging her. Then she screamed, kicking at the soldier. She was so small. He picked her up with one hand and carried his gun in the other. He took her to the gunboats. I never saw her again.

"I did not help my daughter so that I could save my baby. In the end, my baby died anyway. He was already dead on my back where the bullet found him as I ran away from the river, away from my daughter, but I did not know this while I watched the men take her. I would have helped her. I wish I had helped my daughter."

When Rebekah finished telling her story, I felt as if I had fallen into a cesspool. I felt filthy just hearing it. I couldn't imagine what this mother felt seeing it, living it. Or what the daughter felt experiencing it. It was so horrible—disgustingly and humanly inconceivable.

I couldn't imagine living with such memories. Yet somehow, by some mysterious grace, she *was* living with them.

As much as I wanted to turn away from her story—go back to Alabama and wash it off me in the shower of my safe and sequestered home—I knew I could not. For if I turned away from Rebekah's story, I was turning away from Rebekah … and from the daughter she would never see again. And somehow I knew that if I turned away from them, I would be turning away from God. And in turning away from Him, I would be turning away from the part of me that was most human, the part of me that most intimately touched the divine.

It hurt to be there, to look into those faces, to hear those stories. But I knew it would hurt more to turn away.

Chapter 6

STRANDED

I couldn't swim in the cesspool, neither could I climb out. Instead, I began to count the days I had left in Sudan and tried to set my mind on getting home. I simply hoped to survive this horrible experience. I assured myself that once I got home I'd be all right, and I could even send some money to help these poor people.

As the sun rose on the morning we were to fly out of the Shilluk Kingdom, I was the first of our team to walk to the dirt runway. Roasting alone on the airstrip—with no water or shade—another lesson challenged my Western thinking.

Africa runs on her own time and showed no respect for my "early bird gets the worm" mentality. Most of what brought me success or won achievement at home simply didn't work in Africa.

Our schedule said the plane would arrive at 9:00 a.m. By noon the sun was scorching, but it didn't make sense to walk all the way back to camp; I would just dehydrate all the more. Surely, I reasoned, the plane would arrive any minute. I closed my eyes, hoping it would help me to hear the not-too-distant roar of our antiquated potbellied aircraft.

By 2:00 p.m. I gave up and hiked back to base camp. A flush of anger pulsed through me when I saw the men standing around their still-erect tents.

I demanded from our leader, "Why haven't you broken camp, and where is our plane?"

His answer threatened to make me do what I promised myself I would not do in front of these men: break down in tears. The pilot had called our team leader's satellite phone hours earlier to break the news.

Our pilot said he had to turn around; he was headed back to Kenya. Hydraulics trouble. They could fix the plane, but it would take the rest of the day. Between the fighting, dirt runways, and lack of electricity for lighting, no one flies into Sudan at night. It would be tomorrow before they would come for us.

None of us Americans were used to being so out of control. There was no one with whom we could file a complaint or be accommodated, reimbursed, or even consoled. We were all being stretched to meet life as it happened, with nothing to insulate us from its harsh realities.

Resigned to reality, we rationed our water as it was in short supply and steadied ourselves for one more night in the bush.

Taking pity, the village elders brought us a small gazelle for dinner that a local boy caught in his trap. After stringing the still-kicking gazelle up by her feet—on the tree that shaded my tent—the butcher began hacking at the gazelle's long neck.

B-a-a-a-h. b-a-a-a-ah. Staccato bleats filled the air for forty-five minutes while our dinner's blood splashed against my tent, and her head dropped to dangle by a thin string of furry skin.

As darkness veiled us in the mystery of Africa, the men gathered around to resume their man circle—a nightly ritual of "women and war" storytelling from around the globe. One man fought in the Vietnam War, others served in peacetime military efforts. Several of the Sudanese had been child soldiers abducted to fight in both the north and south sides of the Sudanese war. All had their war tales—complete with wives and women—to brag about. And here I sat, a white woman with nothing to say about the spoils of their wars.

I crawled inside my tent, relieved to safely eavesdrop from outside their circle.

The pungent odor that had splashed on my tent in the earlier slaughter drove my mind to fret about how long it would take for some wild, hungry animal to search out what food laid inside my blood-soaked sleeping quarters.

I tossed on top of my sleeping bag most of the night, praying my story would have a "Shadrach, Meshach, and Abednego" ending. I especially prayed for the lions' mouths to be shut and for our plane to be on time in the morning.

Morning finally came. I awoke bleary-eyed, soaked with sweat, and thankful I was one more day closer to home.

Rolling to my side, I tried to cough out the sand that had gathered itself like a wad of sandpaper in the back of my throat. Nothing came out.

I looked at my thermometer: 92 degrees at sunrise. We would easily reach 125 today. How long can a person live without water in this heat? Since women, as a rule, have more body fat than men, I would outlast the men. I wasn't altogether certain that was a good thing.

Once again, I was the first on the airstrip. The day played out exactly as it had the day before. No plane. I cried sitting on the edge of the runway, hanging on the fringe of despair, certain I would never get out of Sudan.

An Intimate Moment

My head pounded from dehydration; I was out of water.

Walking alone back to base camp, I met a tall, beautiful woman on the road coming from the opposite direction. She smiled and cocked her head curiously as she looked me over. We both attempted conversation, but the language barrier made it difficult.

We stood in the heat, exposed to the blistering sun, studying one another. She was the first to raise her hand to my face, slowly seeking permission with her eyes. I stilled myself to show my acceptance of her touch.

Her calloused fingers felt like crocodile hide sliding across my face. She giggled at the softness of my skin, pulled her hand away for the span of time it took her to cluck her tongue against the roof of her mouth, and then covered both my cheeks with the fullness of her thick hands.

Our eyes locked, and immediately I loved this woman. The woman who I could've been. The woman who could've been me. The woman who certainly suffered hunger, war, rape, death of husband and children, simply because of the color of her skin, the spot on the planet she happened to fill, and the fact that she was a woman.

I loved her, and I felt a smidgen of my selfishness slip away. The horrific stories, my loneliness, and facing my fear—with no one present to comfort me—all worked together to melt my mask of security. Sharing a small bit in their suffering helped me move beyond simple compassion for God's broken creatures—to admitting I am one also.

My heart gave a morsel of itself to this strange woman I had met on the road to nowhere.

I touched her face as she had mine. She held her eyes wide open, boring into mine. Her crocodile-skinned hand guided mine down her throat to a scar just above her left breast. She never took her eyes off my face as my eyes studied the scar I now fingered.

Cautioning myself not to recoil at the smell of disease her body carried, I drew close to this tall, gallant woman where I could study her disfigurement.

Bite marks.

I felt nauseous, and again, wanted to run. But to where? There was no place I could run, just like there had been no place this beautiful woman standing before me could have run. I was there to be a witness. It was the only thing I could give her—my presence and willingness to see her, witness what she endured, stand with her, and not turn away.

To be a witness for another seemed like such an insignificant call, and yet I had no idea that it would demand everything within me to learn to do this simple thing.

She pointed to my boots. Unsure as to why, I put my hands out in a confused gesture. Continuing to smile, she bent down and pulled gently at my boot strings. She wanted my boots.

I looked at her feet. She, like Rebekah, wore green rubber flip-flops.

I bent down, unlaced my boots and handed them to her. As she slid her feet from her slippers, my heart stopped for just a moment.

They were Rebekah's. There was no doubt. They had the same perfectly round hole in the exact spot in the heel. Emotion welled within me at the realization that these women shared whatever they had with each other.

If one had a pair of shoes and another did not, when the one without shoes had to walk a long way, the one with shoes would share whatever she possessed. This kind of sacrificial sharing stunned me. They shared not just shoes but a true and faithful sisterhood.

The stranger on the dirt road handed me Rebekah's flip-flops, inviting me to participate in their sisterhood. I pushed my feet into them. Feelings of unworthiness to wear Rebekah's shoes overwhelmed me.

I cried in the dirt road while the woman wrestled her feet into my boots. I knelt before her, lacing the thorn-scarred boots for her.

A woman whose name I would never know towered over me as I knelt at her feet, fumbling with boot laces. Studying my tears, her crocodile-skinned fingers caught one as it dripped down my sunburned cheek, and she rubbed it on her own black face. Not able to find her own tears, she borrowed mine. I prayed somehow they would offer a ray of healing for her suffering heart.

As abruptly as our encounter began, my nameless, tearless friend ended it. Proud of her wares, her face shone as she smiled and waved at me, walking away with her first-ever pair of real shoes.

Giving, and Letting Go

The next twenty-four hours dragged on as we all fretted about not having enough water and if we would ever see an airplane again. Early in the morning, I heard the prop engines roar before I could see the full silver belly of our plane.

In my excitement, I stood too close to the spinning propellers and swallowed mouthfuls of kicked-up dust. After a stern but gentle scolding, the pilot gave me a cardboard box full of plastic water bottles. The tepid water cleared my throat, but burned all the way down.

The men rapidly loaded our plane with tents, bags, and the two motorbikes we used to explore the bush. I sat on the sidelines, taking it all in while guzzling more water. From the corner of my view, a group of too-young and thin soldiers drew my attention. Something was odd. Then I saw it.

This group, whom we aptly called the Flip-Flop Patrol because of the cheap rubber flip-flops they walked and fought in, were clad as expected—except one. The tallest among them wore a pair of thorn-scarred boots. Mine.

My first instinct was to demand that he give them back to me. I had given them to help a woman—my sister whom I loved—alone on the road with a long walk ahead of her. Now what?

Was I to wear flip-flops with a hole in them through the thorny bush of Sudan so that a soldier—who is often guilty of the rapes and mutilations that my sister suffered—could protect his feet with my boots?

As I wrestled with what to do, it occurred to me that this man could be the woman's husband, or maybe she bartered with the boots for food for her family. In the end, I would never know. I'd done what I did in an act extending myself. I chose an act of faith and love. I decided to leave it at that.

We Just *Might* Make It

The pilot had been wrong when he said the mechanic could repair the plane we had originally chartered. The replacement plane was much smaller.

As the men jammed motorbikes between seats in the aisle, my ears perked when I heard two men discussing if the smaller plane would be able to take off with this much weight.

The Vietnam vet was confident we would all be fine. Larry

Warren, president of African Leadership, had Paul and Eddy, his two teenage sons, with him and challenged, "I'm not so sure."

Our pilot meant to assure us, saying, "If we can just clear more runway, we just might make it."

Might?

My eyes grew wide as I watched two Africans extend our runway by drawing out long knives called *pangas* and hack down wild bush at the end of the dirt airstrip.

My mind raced to an event from two weeks earlier when a planeload of missionaries flying into Sudan got sloppy while securing their cargo. The load shifted in midflight, causing the plane to pitch. The pilot lost control of the aircraft. All on board plummeted to their deaths.

"Look!" I said. "I am not getting on that plane! I'd rather take my chances with the Janjaweed than in a plane that you guys hope 'might' be able to take off."

The father sided with me. The vet mocked us both. In the end, one of the bikes and a three-hundred-pound Shilluk man, who was a team guide, remained behind for the next plane, whenever that might be.

The rest of us got on board and headed to Nyamlel in Bahr el Ghazal on the border of Darfur, one of the most godforsaken places on the face of the earth … as I was soon to find out.

Chapter 7

THE A-B-C-D'S OF
COMMITMENT

Finally on the border of Darfur, we confirmed the reports we'd heard of fighting, entire villages burned to the ground, and surviving family members on the run.

Shaken, exhausted, and dehydrated, we walked a couple of dusty miles from the Nyamlel airstrip, hoping to confirm a better report regarding a man from the local Dinka tribe who had a heart for orphans.

I was surprised to find mahogany trees at the cusp of the Sahara Desert. Every few hundred feet, we took comfort in their shade. Looking ahead to a near-perfect triangle of three mahoganies separated by two hundred feet of sand stretching between them, we found our Dinka man. He stood under the tree, which had a chalkboard leaning against it, while a cluster of children gathered around him sitting in the dirt.

"A, B, C, D," he said in a loud voice for all the children to hear.

"A, B, C, D," the children answered in unison.

The children kept repeating "A, B, C, D" loudly, over and over again, while the man ran to the next tree where another cluster of children sat in the dirt.

"One, two, three, four," he chanted, dramatically motioning for the children to repeat.

Again in unison, the children sang out, "One, two, three, four."

On to the next tree the man ran. "For God so loved the world."

"For God so loved the world" came the unified response from the third group.

And the man was off to his first cluster, "E, F, G, H." And on and on he went.

He Gave Up the "Good Life"

Most of our group wandered off to see what more exciting thing might be happening in the village. But a few of us were captivated by children with empty bellies who were even hungrier to learn what this mysterious man offered them.

Those of us who stayed learned the young man's name was James Lual Atak, and he was one of the Lost Boys of Sudan. Lost Boys were homeless orphans whose villages had been burned to the ground, and their families killed.

The Lost Boys walked aimlessly through the desert and jungle of Sudan. They stayed on the move, hoping to avoid wildlife and abduction into the army where they would be placed on the front lines in the bloody five-decade war.

James had been given the opportunity to immigrate to the United States, but he gave up his chance at what he called "the good life" because his heart broke for the younger orphans still in his country.

It seemed he had an abundance of undying passion and unwavering commitment. What he didn't have was financial backing or formal education beyond hit-and-miss classes in sporadic refugee camps.

Alone, James began to gather orphans from the bush and educate them under the trees. Most of the children were sick. All of them were malnourished. None of them had homes. James had no means to help them with these critical needs.

He had exactly 153 orphans. That night I crawled into my tent and opened my Bible, looking for comfort. My hands trembled as I held it up for my headlamp's beam to clear a path through the darkness. I stumbled upon John 21:11, "So Simon Peter went aboard and hauled the net ashore, full of large fish, 153 of them. And although there were so many, the net was not torn."

"Lord, is this why you brought me to Sudan, this hellhole in the world? Is this what all the treacherous travel, pain, and fear have been about—to meet this young man and help him?"

I desperately hoped that God's answer would be something less demanding, something more theoretical, something like, "No, no, My child. I just wanted you to learn some philosophy about life. Now you can go home and rest."

Overwhelmed by my own questions—and hearing no clear answers—I was thankful for the privacy of my tent, where I was free to cry. My head filled with images of malnourished orphans sitting in the dirt, hungry to learn the scrap of numeric and alphabetic wealth James offered them as he ran the Mahogany Triangle.

Gun Running?

Reliving the day from the safety of my tent, I saw little children—five, six, or seven years old—sitting cross-legged in the dirt. Most of them burned with fever from malaria or other ailments for which they had no medicine.

As I walked from cluster to cluster—hearing each lesson—I saw the same scene. One or two children from each huddle would one moment be intent on the lesson, the next bent over—head between knees—vomiting in the span of sand bridging their feet. They'd kick dirt over their vomit and return an intent gaze upon their teacher as if nothing irregular had happened at all.

For them, it hadn't. Being sick, dying even, with no help or comfort was the norm of their day.

I studied their tiny black faces, watched them as they struggled. Never did I see or feel an ounce of self-pity from even one of those children. When the fever got the better of them, they'd simply walk, or crawl, over to the periphery of the mahogany classroom to lay their head on a root of the classroom tree. They took rest for a time and then rejoined their classmates.

Seeking distraction from questions I could not answer and the haunting images in my head, I left my tent to join the man circle.

James called out to our circle: "Hey! I know where there are thousands of Darfurees hiding out in the desert. They are only a few hours from here. Will you go with me tomorrow?"

I'd always heard of African gun running, and I feared James was about to ask us to help him take revenge upon the people of Darfur for all the persecution, genocide, and slavery they had taken part in against his people.

My heart sank.

Someone in the circle responded, "Why would you want us to go to the Darfurees, James?"

"Because, man! They're dying out there! They don't have food, water, or any medicine at all! You've brought so much; we have to take them some of ours!"

Like a fool, I plunged headlong into the conversation. "You

know, Voice of the Martyrs has supplied this food and medicine this one time; it is all you may ever get. When we leave this place, you probably will never hear from any of us again. Help me to understand why you would want your precious supplies to go to the very killers of the parents of the 153 orphans that you are trying to save."

Undaunted, James came at me. "Man! I thought you were Christians! Don't you understand the only real peace for my people is the love of Jesus? We can't just go out there and talk about Jesus. We have to be Jesus to them and take them food, medicine, and help!"

The conversation ended with James's relentless passion. Knowing I'd revealed both my naiveté and selfishness, I sank into silent shame and wished I hadn't slithered out of my tent. Even while fear mounted within me, divine conviction told me James's spirit was genuine. I knew I had to go. Shame for not wanting to go, and anticipation for what the following day would bring, vexed me through the night.

The Scent of Death

The next day, all twenty or so of us loaded up in the open bed of a small Toyota pickup truck, and we headed deeper into Darfur.

Standing up in that open-bed truck as it sped through the bush was the scariest thing I had ever experienced. Until we found the people for which we searched.

Thousands of them.

Mile after mile of refugees, stringing up any stitch of cloth they could find between four hand-broken branches stuck in the ground to make a scrap of shelter from the scorching sun. Men, women, and children alike chased our truck as we penetrated the crowd.

Once our wheels stopped rolling, thousands pushed in around

us. As I climbed out of the truck, riots of people clustered in so tight around us that it was difficult to find a place to plant my feet on solid ground.

I fought for air. The smell of death, disease, and human waste burned at the back of my throat, making me gag. The people were so tall that I couldn't gain high enough ground to draw a fresh breath. I feared I was going to pass out.

I looked at the frail forest of people surrounding me. Legs like saplings struggling for life. Arms like barren branches, reaching out to me. Gaunt cheeks. Sunken eyes. Hair so fragile it broke and fell out if you brushed against it. Swollen bellies full of nothing but worms.

I could not imagine that hell would be worse than this. For the first time in my life, I understood suicide, or even taking the life of my own children, if it meant saving them from a fate like this.

One Little Girl

Just at my claustrophobic worst, when I was ready to bolt, some women brought a little girl to me. Her name was Teresa.

Teresa appeared to be six, perhaps seven. She was severely dehydrated, weak from malnutrition, and infection oozed from her right eye. Beyond that, I couldn't guess what was wrong with her. Malaria? River blindness? Parasitic infection? Who knew?

The women begged me to help. But I had nothing to give her. Only my heart. So I gave her all of what I had. I knelt down beside her and looked into her hollow, yet mysteriously hopeful eyes. "Teresa," I said. "I don't have the good medicine to help you now, but I'm preparing to return to my home, America."

I stopped talking for a moment as all the women punched their fists high into the air, cheering wildly at the sound of "America."

As fists lowered and cheers settled, I continued, "I don't have anything to help you now, but I promise you when I get home, I will tell every person I know and anyone who will listen about you. I will find help, and I will come back to you with the help of many."

Teresa's oozing eyes never left me as I climbed into the bed of our truck. Years later, they are still the ones I find questioning me throughout many sleepless nights.

I wasn't so afraid on the long drive back to our camp; anger and sadness squeezed it out of me. The next morning as we prepared to leave Nyamlel, Larry and I each gave James five thousand dollars. We told him to develop a food program and build some classroom tukels to keep the kids out of the rains when they came.

Larry spoke with James a long while. I listened, watched, and wondered what good ten thousand dollars would do in this living hell.

When I arrived in the United States, I tried as best I could. But in the dozens of times I told her story in the following months, neither the world nor the church seemed to care about Teresa.

By the time I returned to Darfur, Teresa was dead. The women could not tell me what killed her. Probably thirst, they said.

This time, there were no fists punching high in the air. There were no voices cheering America.

I couldn't help but wonder, *Had Teresa died from lack of water ... or from lack of compassion?*

Chapter 8

A YEAR AT HOME

I took a full year at home to do as I had promised—share the story of Teresa's life and death to all who would hear. For me, each time I spoke of Teresa, it was as if she hung onto the frayed thread of life all over again. Her swollen belly—full of nothing but hunger and dysentery—gurgled their complaint, and her sad eyes oozed an infectious cry for help.

Each time, I hoped maybe the audience who heard her story would listen to God's tears flowing through it and be moved to respond to save others like Teresa. But each time, when they did not, I grieved her loss all over again as if she were dying again that very day. Another life lost. Another hope dashed.

I blamed myself a lot, feeling as if I just wasn't telling the story well enough or to enough people. Surely, I thought, if I tried this tactic, or called that person, or visited this church, or prayed harder, worked more, ate and slept less, or *something*—surely, finally, people would see Teresa and come together to save those she left behind. I believed, together, we could make a difference.

I believed saving the lives of helpless children mattered more than just about anything I could imagine. I wanted others to see there was something more important than going to church and coming home to a clean and orderly home.

I began to realize—up until I lost Teresa—that I thought faith was about the joy I reaped from walking with Christ. Teresa showed me living a life of faith starts with knowing the whole heart of God—what brings Him joy, and what breaks His heart. Once I knew both of these things, my life began to keep rhythm with His heartbeat, and I found myself reaching out to the Teresas of our world, just as He would.

It seemed that, aside from working to save helpless children myself, the most important thing I could do with my life was to help *other* people also know God's heart—particularly for orphans—and find their personal steps to the music of His heart. At first, living so close to the pain of our world wasn't easy. I roused most nights from nightmares filled with violent images I was afraid to face in my waking hours. In one recurring dream my eyes swelled with infection. Puss oozed from my tear ducts and dried on my lashes, matting them shut. Unable to see, I spun round and round trying to feel my way out of the horde of people pushing in around me, suffocating me with the smell of death they carried. Hands clawing at my eyes and ripping out clot-sealed lashes jolted me from sleep. The offending hands were my own.

By day, I wondered what the dream meant. What was the true offense of my hands? What couldn't I see? To what was I blind? What was I missing? Perhaps, I thought, it was something that, had I seen it in time, I would have been able to move people fast enough to save Teresa. I had failed to save her, and in my sleep, the features and colors that distinguished her face from mine blurred. In my dreams we often traded places—Teresa's life for mine.

I felt angry over the disparate nature of my life and Teresa's. She'd been robbed of dignity even in her death. When my time came, I would probably be hospitalized in a sterile, safe, painkiller-stocked hospital where death would be ushered in as quietly and gracefully as a waltz. By contrast, Teresa's death lacked even the eloquence of an epileptic seizure.

Agonizing Contrasts

Every fiber of my being resisted slipping comfortably back into my safe, climate-controlled environment where abundant water quenched my thirst, filled my tub, flushed my waste, and even offered an endless array of recreation. I felt ashamed that I'd failed to deliver the same good life—or any life at all—to Teresa.

I'd once taken for granted the close-knit family I had, with healthy children and a devoted husband who laid down his life for mine many times over. Learning how rare a gift these things really were, I felt guilty about such extravagance.

At times, I couldn't even allow myself to rest in Milton's loving arms because of the sadness I felt for how exposed Teresa, her mother, and millions of others were. Stepping outside my safe environment, I felt the plight of the world so overwhelmingly that I couldn't reconcile their suffering with my blessing.

My discomfort, though, solved little. It didn't bring Teresa back. It didn't save other children. It all seemed so futile. I couldn't enjoy the life I'd once known, and yet my suffering accomplished nothing. I longed to find a way to make Teresa's life and death make a difference for other children who still clung to the frayed thread of hope that snapped precisely where Teresa held.

Teresa's death became a living thing swelling within me. Feeding on my broken heart, it grew, transforming me along the way into an intercessor for the forgotten children Teresa represented.

Fighting Demons Together While Miles Apart

Meeting Teresa changed the way I understood my life, my purpose. Losing her drove me to search for ways to do for other children what

I had not been able to do for Teresa. My love for Teresa, and the stretching of it to cover other children, was a good emotion. My broken heart for their suffering was a beautiful thing.

The problem was, up to my first trip to Sudan, Milton and I had cried tears for injustice together. Our combat against oppression had been fought side by side, covering each other's back, sharing each other's burden, and bearing witness to each other's pain.

Make Way Partners had been birthed from our joint broken hearts for the abused African children we found in Portugal. God called both of us to this work, and we assumed we were forever intertwined in the battle.

By the time I went to Sudan, Milton's health had grounded him to work stateside. With his escalating diabetes and decreasing stamina, suddenly I was thrust to the front lines—alone. I felt vulnerable with my protective partner-shield ripped from me. I experienced life-altering events without Milton, and he couldn't quite grasp what I was going through.

Milton was left to struggle with himself. He wrestled with questions about his masculinity—specifically with the protector he was hardwired to be, yet now seemed to be sidelined.

I worried about Milton's health and how I would be able to lead Make Way Partners if diabetes robbed me of him altogether. Wanting to protect him from extra stress that I feared would impact his health, I began to shield Milton from my worst fears, darkest nightmares, and many painful things that I experienced while in Sudan.

I didn't realize I was losing him by the distance I created, one secret at a time.

We stammered around, cautiously trying to express what each

of us faced. One day Milton told me, "John Eldredge says in *Wild at Heart* that the question men most struggle with is 'Do I measure up?' Well, for me, sending you out there alone makes me ask 'Am I man enough? Can I still even protect myself, much less you, my children, and our home?'"

I'd always seen Milton as larger than life. So full of energy, libido, and passion that, in my mind, there was nothing he couldn't do and no one he couldn't protect me from.

Hearing Milton's pain—seeing how fragile his disease made him feel—I became even more guarded in what I shared with him. I was afraid if I shared how vulnerable, alone, and scared I felt, it would only cause him to question himself more. The more I tried to protect Milton from my struggles—the more I tried to carry them alone— the thicker the barrier between us grew.

The hard and high wall that kept me from spilling over onto him also blocked him from being able to reach into me and draw out what he needed from his wife.

Reality Check in the Church Environment

As we fought to find our bearings in this new landscape, a mega- church in Birmingham invited the two of us to speak. We felt excited because the one piece of our work we still shared was a passion to help mobilize the church outside her four walls.

The inviting church already financially supported Make Way Partners and thought they wanted their people to know more about the ministries and missionaries they funded. We were scheduled to speak in various adult Sunday school classes throughout the church— one class at a time—spread out over several Sundays. Milton and I were once again united and excited about the opportunity to speak for the voiceless.

We worked diligently on putting together an appropriate version of how God called us to protect the most vulnerable children in the world. The story, of course, had to include our eye-opening experience in Portugal.

Remembering how shocking the mass rapes and trafficking of innocent women and children were when we first saw and heard about them, we took great pains to be sensitive to our audience as we shared our story. We gave only enough information for people to understand the nature of what the children suffered, without being so graphic as to overwhelm our listeners or further exploit the children.

Our second Sunday into the commitment, a deacon and Sunday school teacher invited us to lunch. After a pleasant meal, he walked us outside to deliver the distasteful news: "I'm sorry to have to tell you this, but some of the women in our classes are very upset by the things you are sharing. One lady even told me, 'If this is the kind of depressing thing I'm going to have to listen to when I come to church, then I don't think I want to come.' I am sure you understand that we can't have that. Can we? So, I'm sorry, but I have to ask you not to come back."

The man didn't even wait to hear our response. With head hung low and shoulders slouched, he slowly skulked turtle-like across the parking lot back to his car.

Milton was furious. I was brokenhearted. Did no one want to hear; did no one want to relieve the cry of hopeless children? Doubts and discouragement haunted us both. It seemed we'd been robbed of the last piece of work we could share. We feared we'd made a mistake, misheard God, stepped out too far.

Every time we tried to talk about our compounding losses, Milton grew angrier and I cried harder. We stopped talking about our work.

We smoothed things over by rationalizing that the load the other carried was heavy enough without adding our own to it. But I think the deeper reason we stopped talking was we both feared the intensity of our own pain and anger. We were afraid it might have the power to destroy us. What we didn't understand was that it did—and would—if we tried to bury it.

For the next year or so, the church continued to send a small monthly support check, but they could not force themselves to share the emotional, physical, or spiritual burden of facing the evil we fought. They were willing to fund our storming of hell's rusted gates as long as we didn't ask them to share in the suffering … or paint for them the emotional pictures that fueled our passion. Because money follows the heart, eventually even the monthly checks came to an end.

Forsaken by Others

As the year dragged on, our problems seemed to proliferate. Many of our friends and longtime supporters of the student ministry we led in Spain couldn't understand why we left a "happy ministry" and threw ourselves into such "scandalous" work.

We took comfort in knowing Jesus left glory to live in the poverty of this fallen world, among us broken, scandalous sinners, and He asked us to follow Him. We stayed in the Scriptures of caring for the oppressed, especially Isaiah and Matthew 25. But still, feeling forsaken by friends and supporters was tough going.

We felt God had taken us to Europe specifically to reveal His plan for our lives. I figured He knew I would've run like Jonah had He told me up front that He wanted me to fight the sex-slave trade—especially in the sewers of Bucharest and the desert of Sudan.

We found no comfort in church. Most of the churches we visited focused on salvation, forgiveness, Bible studies, and doing good works—almost exclusively programmatic things taking place within their four walls. We could find none that taught about the reality of extreme poverty, how vulnerable those conditions made women and children to trafficking, or about a biblical response required from the church.

I tried to tell myself not to be so sad or angry. After all, until I was faced with Carlos a few years earlier, I didn't know about trafficking either. My self-talk didn't help much; I still couldn't understand how—once they knew—so many could turn away.

At one time, going to church provided a deep sense of joy and comfort. Now, I felt more alone in the center of a beautiful worship service with glorious music rocking the rafters than I did as the only white woman in the middle of the Sahara Desert surrounded by a mob of hungry, thirsty, smelly, sick, and dying people.

Torn in So Many Ways

I longed to return to Africa and at the same time felt guilty because I knew Milton could not go with me. How could I admit I'd rather be in the Sahara Desert than with him? I felt unfaithful to admit such things, so I kept them to myself where they fostered confusion and loneliness.

Milton was fighting his own battles alone and in silence.

We both worked hard at being responsible with the part and parcel we'd each been dealt; it seemed the only thing we could do. Yet, while doing all the right things, something of our hearts began to die as we labored under a load we were never meant to carry alone.

Little did we realize that squirreling away our darkest pain set us up for facing a white squall so loud and high it would threaten to pull us completely apart, sinking our lives, marriage, and ministry to the depths of the sea of ruin.

By the time my year at home came to a close, I had given up on the church ever listening, or my marriage ever having the intimacy it once covered me in. Whitney and Olivia were both off at college, and I ran back to Africa where I hoped at least I could feel at home again.

Chapter 9

278 TO 2

The last time I had seen James, I had given him a measly five thousand dollars. I figured he held high hopes I would become a regular supporter. I went on believing that for a year—until I showed up again in Sudan and James met me at the plane.

Three days of flying just to arrive in Darfur made me tired and fuzzy-headed. Even after the pilot cut the engine and I stood outside on the folding cockpit ladder, the clatter of the rickety little chartered plane still roared in my ears. I could hear only about half of what James said. Yet, I understood everything because I could feel his surprise, joy, hope, and excitement as my foot hit the last rung of the broken ladder.

James whisked me up into his arms before I touched the desert floor. He hugged me so tightly I thought he might break a rib. When he set my feet on the dusty ground, his viselike grip clamped onto my shoulders.

"I can't believe you came back! You were so afraid the first time, and you barely talked at all. I never thought I'd see you again. I thought you hated Sudan."

Taken aback, I said, "What? Hated Sudan? No. Why would you think that? God has knit a love in my heart for you and your people. I've spent my last year telling everyone I know and anyone who would listen about you, what you are doing, and what we need to do to help you save and protect the orphans."

"You never talked with me. When you came before, all the men sat and talked with me for many hours at night, but you always went directly to your tent very early. I thought you didn't like me or Sudan. I thought you didn't care to hear my stories or what my people suffer."

"Oh, James! I'm so sorry! Of course I care, and of course I want to hear your stories and learn all about your people. Actually, I did hear most of your stories. Every night when you men gathered in your man circle, I just didn't know where I fit. I was the only woman. I was afraid if I sat out late into the nights with all of you, someone might get the wrong idea about me. I was just trying to be careful.

"Besides, you men were talking of women, war, fighting, and killing. What could I possibly say? But my tent was very near, and I listened to your laughter, lies, and stories until you all climbed into your own tents."

"Lies? You think we lied? Well, yes. I could tell some of the men were lying. But me? Never. I am a man of truth!"

At that even James could no longer keep a straight face. We both broke into laughter, slapping each other on the shoulder—almost like the men do—and, in that instant, our relationship was forever changed.

It hit me hard to consider that how little I had spoken to James communicated a lack of both courage and compassion. James was desperate, not first and foremost for money, but to be seen. He needed a witness to his life—of what he'd suffered and what God was doing through him.

He also needed encouragement. The roar in my ears muffled the rest of James's words, but I could tell that while I'd been wrong in thinking I left him with any hope this last year, my return was making up for it in spades.

James Calling

During the year apart from James, while I was in the United States, James had taken it upon himself to call me weekly from his satellite phone. At first, he called to tell me how he was using the money Larry and I had given him. Over time, the phone calls became more conversational and simply about his life and work.

Satellite phones can be a terrific lifeline in times of trouble when there is no other form of contact with the outside world. They work by bouncing signals back and forth between the phone and a satellite, eliminating the need for towers that wouldn't remain standing in a war zone. Powered by small solar panels, they don't even require electricity. However, they can also be quite frustrating with long delays between the time a word is spoken on one end and received on the other.

The very nature of the static-packed delays in James's weekly phone calls helped to fill in the many gaps in my understanding of life in Sudan. The patience it required to communicate one complete thought through the static interference often made me think of how challenging it was to accomplish a simple task like finding enough food to eat, such as one bowl of grain or gruel per day. Our phone calls filled me with stories and information and made me hungry to return.

Week by week, he gave me death reports of "his" orphans—the children he spent his life to save. One day when I picked up my phone, I took note that James greeted me by calling me "Mama

Kimberly." That same conversation was the first time he called them "our orphans," and they've been "ours" ever since.

A year of weekly phone calls from James recounting "a day in the life of saving—and losing—orphans" grew my heart from wanting to save just Teresa to an overwhelming compulsion to spend my life in the same battle. Nothing else seemed as important. James became my Mordecai calling me Mama Kimberly instead of Esther and telling me, "Who knows? Perhaps you were born for just this one thing."

Orphans Need More Than a School

By the time I returned to Sudan, our school had swelled to more than three hundred orphans, and we were feeding them two meals each day. The year before, I'd noticed the children's hair was brittle with a tinge of orange, and their skin looked as if a chalky paste had been patted on them. A doctor told me these were signs of malnutrition, which was understandable when they only received a single meal in a day. Two meals may not have been enough to fatten them up, but the natural black sheen I expected to see in African children was returning!

Our biggest problem was trying to keep the orphans safe at night. We had only a few tukels for school rooms, and most of our classes were still outside under the trees. We had nowhere for them to sleep safely. We lost some every week.

When I told my board of directors about this, they asked for more details. They specifically wanted to know how many orphans died due to lack of housing.

It was a hard task. Knowing children were dying was one thing. Keeping a daily tally was another—especially as I saw their health improving.

The only way to track the information my board wanted was to keep a death census. We counted dead orphans from January through October. In that ten-month period, we lost 278 orphans. The number-one cause of death was not thirst, not malnutrition, not disease. It was animal attacks, mostly by wild dogs or hyenas.

To keep from being eaten in the night, many of our homeless orphans slept in trees. Tragically, some of them fell from their bed branches to their deaths.

No More Walloping for Peter

One evening just before sunset James and I walked through the bush digesting our day and dreaming of what we'd do if we had more funding, food, medicine, and shelter, when we came upon a woman walloping a little boy.

James and I both rushed in to stop the beating. James grabbed the woman's arms and held them down at her sides. She railed against him like a rabid animal, screaming and shouting, while her eyes raced wildly in search of a way out of his grasp. I recognized the little boy as Peter Atak, a boy from our school.

Thrashing in fits of fury, she yelled her justification for beating the small hunkered boy crying at her feet. She said Peter wanted to go to the river for bathing when instead she needed him to gather food for her family.

She derided him with harsh Dinka words I did not understand, but the anger and hate transcended my language barrier.

James picked up the small, thin boy, stood him on his own feet, and bolstered his shoulders to steadiness. Tears streamed down Peter's little dirt-crusted face. Eyes appearing larger than normal in a malnourished, too-small head searched James's face. They offered both love and gratitude.

James told me, "Peter is a very good boy. He was one of the first to come to our school. He has been faithful every day. And he is really very clever. We will take him with us this very night."

A budding father figure, James helped Peter get a bath. Then I sat long into the night talking with Peter. I struggled with what conversation to make with a small boy who'd already suffered more trauma than I could possibly imagine.

I asked him, "Peter, you are about nine years old, and the New Life Ministry School has only been here for a few years. What did you do as a little boy before James started the school?"

Peter's face lit up as he told me, "Oh, Mama Kimberly, my friends and I used to go out into the bush and look for wild animals we could eat. But we had such a hard time killing them, sometimes we would get wild dogs to kill the game for us. But then we had another problem. We had to beat the dogs off of the kill so that we could eat it before the dog did! Now, you and Pastor James feed us every day, and we don't even have to kill for it!"

I relished in Peter's stories for hours until finally I noticed him beginning to nod between his own sentences. With a love I'd never felt for a child, save my own, I led him to the food-storage tukel where James prepared a mat on the floor for him.

William, a Friend for Peter

The next day, James took in another orphan boy from our school, Peter's best friend, William Deng. William slept on a mat next to Peter in the food-storage tukel. I slept on my cot outside their door where I drifted to sleep listening to them happily chattering away like the rodents with whom they shared their new home.

I slept with a large stick on the ground beside my cot. Many a night, I awakened to the rustling sound of wild dogs or hyenas pushing their way through our brittle dried-grass fence. They would come seeking something—or someone—to eat.

I would roll off my cot, grab my stick as I got up, and take off running after the beasts, shouting like a threatening banshee to chase them away. When I could no longer hear them, I would collapse once again on my cot. Each time I returned, the night air carried a thin whisper to me from Peter: "Thank you, Mama. Here in my new house, I don't have to worry about the hyenas anymore. I love you."

The boys fought, played, healed, and grew together as any birth siblings would do. I noticed no matter what boyish insults they hurled at each other during the day, when darkness returned, they were blood brothers against their fears once again.

I never forgot the orphans "out there," the ones still sleeping in the bush; but at least I could tuck my boys in bed at night and go to sleep knowing I'd played some small role in saving two. That mattered to me, and I knew it mattered to God.

Fencing Out Evil

Two years passed between my first trip to Sudan and when we brought and installed a chain-link fence from Nairobi. It was our first step toward any kind of security for the fifty acres we hoped to turn into an oasis for our lost and lonely orphans. Soon afterward, we hired a twenty-four-hour, armed-security-patrol squad. We all slept much better without wildlife running through our camp!

Shortly after we put up our fence, something—I never under-stood exactly what—set the local witches against us. Night after night they crowded around our fence, piercing the quiet darkness with curses against James and me. Some wanted the orphans to become their slaves; others were just pure evil and hated any good God would do or anyone who did good in His name.

One night the cursing raged louder and longer than usual, and it frightened Peter and William in their tukel. The three of us sat on my cot, praying together until the night grew silent again.

The following morning, we three agreed that just before sunset each evening we'd walk around the entire perimeter of our new fence and pray. As we walked, we praised God for who He is, the mighty Host He created, friendship, food, laughter, love, and for all things that came to our hearts.

We confessed where we were conscious of our failing Him. We thanked Him for His many provisions. We asked Him for pro-tection. We also asked Him to supply the needs of the ministry, to raise up strong leaders, and to give us strength and courage to cast out the many oppressive forces and strongholds that worked against us.

We prayed for the witches who wanted to hurt us, and we prayed for the Arabs who wanted to enslave us.

What surprised me about our prayer walks was how eager the boys were. I knew that a slow, prayerful pace would require about an hour's worth of walking. I asked them not to talk to each other or me, but just to the Lord. I told them they could pray in their minds, hearts, and aloud—whatever they wished.

I expected that by the time we made the first corner of our

security fence, Peter and William would be asking me questions, picking at each other, or running off with a passerby playmate.

I was wrong. Within the first few steps, William was the first to start vociferously praising God! He remained several paces behind me, yet I could hear him prattling on and on with God as if they were walking in tandem. Imagine that! Peter's tempo was several steps behind William's, yet I was conscious of his quiet, earnest conversation with his Lord.

A Tough Walk for Peter

One night, as we turned the last corner and began the final stretch of our walk, Peter said to me, "Mama Kimberly, here comes my mother." I looked ahead and saw three women approaching us from a distance of about a hundred feet.

"Your mother? I thought she was dead."

"No. She is not dead; she is the woman that you and James saved me from the night she was beating me in the field."

"I thought the woman beating you was your auntie. She was your mother? Which one is she?"

Peter talked as the few feet between us and the three women closed. "She is the one carrying the newborn baby. She was angry because I didn't fetch enough water, and I couldn't find any food for her. I looked and looked, but there wasn't any. She is not dead; she was beating me because she didn't want me anymore. That is when you and James took me from her and brought me to New Life Ministry."

"Are you going to greet her, Peter?"

"Yes. I want to greet her; I haven't seen her in two years. She is my mother."

Peter's mother stood inches from him as she called out to me, "Mama Kimberly!" She tacked on a slew of Dinka words, which I did not understand.

All smiles, she proudly unveiled the papoose on her body; the child was beautiful. I watched Peter tentatively rub his index finger across his baby brother's face.

Peter slid his hand inside the sheet to fully cup the baby's face and stroke his full cheek as he withdrew it. Holding his hand in midair, he looked at his mother as if considering touching her face as well.

Even after the brutal beatings and complete abandonment, Peter's eyes were full of hopeful expectation as he looked at his mother's face.

Before Peter could make up his mind what to do with his hand, his mother turned and said something to the woman on her right. Then, in unison, the three of them cackled a sort of mocking laughter as they moved past us, leaving Peter alone with his broken hope.

It Is What It Is

That was it. The exchange was over. Peter's mother did not touch her son. The woman did not speak to him. She didn't even look at him.

I searched Peter's face, which expressed what I can only call resigned sorrow. He didn't fight. He accepted his mother as she was. He met his culture on its terms. He lived life and met circumstances as they came to him. He was full of sorrow, yet even at his tender age he knew there was nothing more he could do.

"The Arabs killed my father," Peter finally said as we began slowly walking again.

"I'm so sorry, Peter. And I'm sorry that your mother beat you and didn't want you. You know, you are a very special boy. On that first night, James told me that you are a very good boy and that you are quite clever."

His eyes full of fragile hope, Peter asked, "Are you my mother now?"

"No, I am not your mother. But I love you very much, and I am very thankful that I get to be one of the people God brought to care for you, along with James and all the people who love you here at New Life Ministry."

"What about me, Mama Kimberly? Both of my parents are dead. Are you my mother now?" William asked.

"No, William, I am not your mother either, but just as with Peter, I am very thankful you are in my life, and I get to share in your life. You, too, are very special."

Peter was the one who began praying aloud this time, although it was softer. I couldn't make out exactly what he was saying, but I knew it was a holy dialogue.

I prayed the rest of our walk in silence, thanking God for the two man-boys flanking me. After a few days, the witches stopped assaulting us with their nightly curses, but we enjoyed our prayer walks too much to give them up.

Committing to the Impossible

Losing 278 orphans during our ten-month death census was a hard lesson in counting the cost of not providing housing for our orphans. The healing we saw in Peter and William as they received consistent care offered a sweet encouragement to make room for more orphans.

So together with mourning the loss of 278 and the joy of saving two, we committed ourselves to do what had never been attempted: the impossible task of building the first orphanage available for Darfur refugee orphans where they would share a home with the southern Sudanese orphans.

Both sets of orphans were innocent survivors of genocide. Both sets had seen their parents persecuted, raped, and/or killed by the other's people. Both craved the security of a loving home. By God's grace, we hoped against hope to offer it.

The sheer logistics of building a safe home in a war zone with no infrastructure was God-sized in and of itself. Housing orphan survivors from both sides of a five-decade-long genocidal war where children as young as six years old vowed to kill one another in revenge of their parents would definitely take me beyond my own strength and courage, if the logistical end didn't do it first.

Chapter 10

A LESSON IN HUMILITY

The beautiful healing budding in Peter and William—combined with the devastating results of our death census—convinced us we had to take on what everyone declared as the impossible. We had to build an orphanage to house and protect our children.

We plowed forward and soon learned our commitment alone didn't resolve the many conflicts of the daunting task before us. Never had anyone attempted to provide orphan care in this region. There was no blueprint to follow. No model of success. No culturally sanctioned tradition. We were also nearly two thousand miles from our nearest supply chain: Nairobi, Kenya. Those two thousand miles boasted three miles of pavement, no real roads, and a motherload of bandits.

I've lived in Asia, the Caribbean, Spain, Portugal, and the Appalachian Mountains. I've spent significant time in Africa and Eastern Europe. Yet the five decades of Islamic invasion, slavery, persecution, famine, and disease that is unique to Sudan has birthed and fostered a hopelessness I've never quite encountered anywhere else in the world.

The war and genocide has left Sudan with nine women for every one man. There are more widows and orphans than any other people group. Who remains to care for the country's orphans?

It borders on the absurd to expect a widow to save another's orphan from the same starvation, rape, disease, or slavery that has taken five out of her own six children. Orphan care is such a foreign thought that locals even create folklore to justify the abandonment.

The legend goes like this: If a mother dies in childbirth, she calls her baby from the grave because mother and newborn cannot be separated. Anyone, then, who offers care to the newborn is guilty of keeping mother and child apart and will receive the worst curse of all the witches.

Sometimes these babies are thrown into the river. Sometimes they are left unkempt in their afterbirth and fecal matter—alone in a dark tukel—waiting for the death call of their mothers to carry them to her arms on the other side.

The Steep Hills of Battle

On one hand, I definitely believe that Christ transcends all time and culture; and He presents Himself in relative ways to the entire world. On the other hand, we also know that no culture is pure, and all cultures have developed sinful habits or coping mechanisms to justify what they want or think they need. There's a fine line between trying to Westernize a culture with our own mores and standing idly by while life is wasted or oppressed.

Working to present a Kingdom culture, rather than fighting against the culture you're in or defending your own, is genuinely a humbling challenge. I was about to get a mouthful of humbling.

Dangerous distance, bandits, slavery, and genocide were about all a donor had to hear before he lost interest in a project, even for orphans. Add that to our puny organizational size and an even smaller bank balance and we looked laughable. No one believed in us, and many openly told us we were doomed to failure.

Many other complications threatened our determination. For example, we had to get our own trucks and drivers to haul in everything we needed. Everything. There were no Wal-Marts, Home Depots, furniture stores, grocery stores, or pharmacies. Five decades of war rendered commerce impossible in Sudan; we had to bring all supplies from home or Kenya.

After acquiring the trucks and drivers, we calculated how long it would take the rivers to recede at the end of the rainy season, then get the trucks rolling and secure to their destination before the next season's rain began filling them up again. That's no exact science, but it's a real deal-breaker if not planned accurately.

At best, our trucks would travel along dirt-packed trails, plowing their way through the thick, thorny bush. At worst, the many bandits and rebels who stalked the dirt roads would ambush the trucks, seize all our supplies, and perhaps kill our drivers.

I worked for months in the States scrounging up the funds to get us started. Five decades of war also rendered construction a lost art in Sudan, so James used his time to recruit construction workers from Kenya. We would partner each Kenyan with Sudanese laborers who could learn a new trade, and together they would build our orphanage.

Funds barely dripped into our bucket; not many caught the vision for building in a war zone. The next rainy season was fast approaching, and we knew with no roads or bridges we would not be able to cross the country once the rains began. We had to start in a month's time or delay a whole year.

I flew back to Nairobi to meet James with the funds and to document our progress. We signed contracts in Nairobi for supplies to be delivered as cash on delivery once the goods arrived in Nyamlel. Then James and I flew to Sudan to recruit Sudanese laborers and prepare for the ground breaking.

It was harder work than I thought. Locals simultaneously doubted we would follow through on all that we promised and feared that we would. Their biggest fear seemed to be ground in suspicion of why we would invest so much money to save African orphans.

Complications in Getting Supplies

In the midst of the local hostility, I often felt like a small flame on a dark, windy night. A glimmer of hope among a hopeless people can be like a blazing torch that will guide you safely out of the dark, or reveal to your enemy where you are hiding. When you first set the torch afire, you have no way of knowing which it will be.

At the end of a day so long it seemed we crammed three days into it, James and I had one final task on our list before crashing for the night. As we dropped into our plastic chairs, James powered up his satellite phone to check on our drivers' safety and whereabouts.

All the potential mistakes, miscalculations, and hazards, along with nature's unpredictability, wore on me. James seemed to take it all in stride.

Before James could dial the convoy's satellite number, his sat phone rang. I braced myself, somehow knowing the news would not be good. James spoke in Kiswahili to Munene, our lead truck driver and logistician, on the other end of the phone. I could only understand enough to confirm we had a problem.

James stood, paced, thrashed his hand in the air, and raised his voice. He was no longer "in stride." My anxiety grew with every gesture, every inflection, every increase in volume.

Hitting the phone's off button, James turned to me.

"Mama, our trucks were attacked. Munene's sidekick Ibrahim

was beaten, and the soldiers threatened to kill him. Two of the drivers grew so afraid that they fled back to Kenya."

"We had four trucks," I answered. "What about the other two? Did they run? Where are they?"

James's voice was heavy. "Only two remain faithful. Munene and Ibrahim are free now, and still they remain on our side."

"This is good," I said, relieved. "At least some of our supplies will come. We can make do."

"Yes. It is good. But we still have one problem. The waters are not yet gone down all the way from last year's rain, so another river has grabbed our trucks. Our two remaining trucks are stuck. Our drivers have run out of food. They have no money so the villagers around them will not help. Our drivers are hungry and sick. They will not survive long without our help."

"Where are they?"

James's face relaxed, and his shoulders dropped. "Oh, Mama, they are not far at all! We will go to them tomorrow morning on my dirt bike. I will go now to find diesel somewhere for the journey."

"Journey? How far?"

"Not far at all, at all. We can make it in two hours' time, give Munene and Ibrahim money for food, and return all in the same day."

Mzee, Wise Old Man

I was horrified at the thought of riding through the bush on the back of a motorcycle, hours away from base camp, alone with James. "But, James, I don't think I really need to go. If you are just going to be gone a few hours, I will be fine here, working with the children and recording testimonies."

"*No!* That won't do at all, at all! I promised Milton the *mzee* [local word for 'wise old man'] that I would watch over you and keep you safe. It is too dangerous for me to leave you alone here for an entire day. I told the mzee I would die before I would let anything happen to you, and a man does not break his word to a mzee. You must remain with me."

The promise James referred to was one he had made to Milton as he prepared to release me to go into Sudan for months at a time. Being an insulin-dependent diabetic with organ damage drove Milton to face his own limitations and mortality. It did not prepare him to face mine.

For that, he would have to wrestle with God day and night. Fear, anger, loss, doubt, attempts to negotiate and control would all wriggle their way through him—launched at both God and me— until finally, like Jacob at the end of a long night's wrestling, he let me go.

This letting go did not come, though, until he had James on the satellite phone promising to watch over me and do everything in his might to keep me safe. Few men know the stripping away of self that it takes to turn the life of their wife over to another. While Milton knew ultimately I was in God's hands, he did everything he could on his watch to make a safe path for me.

When Milton took me to the airport for that first long trip into Sudan, he held my hands, bore his eyes into mine, and said, "From this moment on, I count you as dead until God returns you to me or reunites us after this life." Those became the last words he would say to me each time he released me.

I was learning the hard way that things we sort out at home

rarely prove effective in Sudan. What my loving husband intended for good—making James promise to watch over me—put me in more peril than he could have imagined, for James felt as though he could never leave my side. His feelings of responsibility to watch over the "White Woman" in his charge had no boundaries.

I knew Milton would not want me to get on that bike. I also knew his concerns were wise because if something happened to James on the journey, I had few African-style survival skills and doubted I would live to tell the tale.

Yet, James wouldn't go unless I did, and our faithful drivers were desperate for help. There was no one else, no backup plan. I decided to risk it.

I Can't Believe I'm Doing This

Long after the sun went to bed—and James should have—he went looking for diesel. I thrashed on my cot wondering what in the world I had gotten myself into.

Shortly after sunrise, James got on the motorbike and handed me a billy club. He modeled for me how to use it to bash the head of any human or animal that might chase us as we raced through the bush.

An ankle I'd broken in a dirt-bike accident two months earlier was barely healed. The tenderness of that break kept me mindful of the danger of the journey ahead. Still, a bike wreck was not my worst fear. That was saved for the Janjaweed.

While climbing on the back of the bike, a singular thought snaked through my mind: *I can't believe I'm doing this.*

I wasn't sure where to put my hands. I had always been careful about physical boundaries with James so it didn't feel right to put my arms around him. I put my hands on top of his shoulders, gripping hard.

Shortly after getting out of the village and deep into the bush, I stuck my head out to the side to look around James and up the road. I saw the first pack of wild dogs waiting for us on the side of the road as if we were an on-schedule *matatoo* (African-style van/bus).

Fear gripped me, squeezing proper etiquette out of me; I pushed my body so tightly against James that the sweat on his back soaked through my shirt.

He yelled at me, "Get ready! You must beat the wild dogs with the stick I gave you, or else they will bite us, and we don't have the rabies shot!"

I was afraid to lunge after them. I anchored myself to James by wrapping my arms around his middle and holding the stick tightly in both hands, clutched in front of his chest.

Again James yelled, "Kimberly! You have to hit them! Do you want to wreck and be eaten alive out here in the desert? What about the mzee? I promised to keep you safe. Get ready! Raise your stick, woman!"

"Woman?" I didn't like the way he was talking to me.

A rush of anger ousted the fear in me long enough to let go of James, raise the billy club over my head, and scream out like some wild, injured thing. Swinging the club fiercely, I felt the crack of bone as it smashed into skull after skull.

Losing one or two didn't seem to deter the pack; there were so many, and they just kept coming. My scream dropped lower from my throat into a lioness-like growl as I kicked at them with my boot, as well.

Finally, the dogs fell behind as James sped through the bush. James threw his head back in laughter that cackled on the edge of crazy. Through his howls, I heard him say, "You did it, Kimberly! I didn't know you were such a tough woman, but I am learning it is true. I see you really are a very strong woman. Ooo! I tell you, I wouldn't want you to be angry with me, Mama!"

From Bad to Worse

I may have managed to impress James with my "toughness," but four hours into our "two-hour ride," my back throbbed miserably.

I told James, "I'm getting tired, and my back hurts. In a few minutes, I will need to take a rest."

"Sure. Sure. We will stop soon."

He revved the engine, and we tore through the bush. The bush, in turn, tore through me, its three-inch thorns raking my scalp. The sun baked the blood in my hair, matting it in large sections for the thorns to snag and rip chunks from my head.

My tailbone turns slightly outward and tends to break through my skin if I sit too long, or in the wrong position. My chiropractor believes I broke it when I was a child, and it never healed properly. Acute pain wore on me.

The motorbike seemed to find every rut, every hole, as I flounced around on the back, holding on for dear life. The pain was sharp and climbed higher up my spine. When I could bear it no longer, I called out again. "James, remember I need to stop soon."

"Fine. Fine. Yes, we will stop very soon."

On we rode, more than five hours into our two-hour journey. James's trunklike legs suddenly jetted out from the bike like oversized kickstands as he bogged in the sand, nearly jettisoning me from the bike.

My lower back twisted and sent shockwaves of pain all the way up to my neck.

"Stop this stinkin' bike right this minute!"

Alarmed, James stopped. I jumped off the bike and yelled. "I've been telling you for hours that I need a break! My back hurts. I'm tired. I'm thirsty. I'm hungry! And you haven't even been listening to me!"

As if he'd never heard me say that I needed to rest, he said, "Oh, I am so sorry. I didn't know. I thought you were having a good time with me. I thought we were doing fine. We haven't even had a wreck yet or anything. We are nearly there."

At my breaking point, I blasted James with both barrels.

"*Nearly there?* You've been telling me that for hours! You told me it would only take us two hours, and we have been on that *stupid* bike *all stinkin' day!* You said we'd be back at base camp before dark. It is getting dark already and you can't even find our trucks! You keep circling the same blasted bush trying to find your way out, my head gets ripped wide open every time you plow under a thorn tree. *You've* got a helmet! *Your* head isn't the one getting torn up! Besides that, you don't even know where you are! You are lost!"

"Kimberly. Please. You would be better to calm down. I am so sorry. I don't want to disappoint you. You can wear my helmet; I just thought I should have it because I am the driver. Just get back on the bike; I will get us there. You pray, and I promise that God will show us the way."

I drew a deep exaggerated breath, and then exhaled with

groaning regrets for my outburst. "No. It is me who is sorry. I shouldn't be yelling at you. Forgive me. Of course, I don't want your helmet. You must be able to hold your head up to see while we maneuver this torturous bush. I just need to rest a few minutes. Then, we'll go."

We sat in silence. At least I did. James began in silence but somewhere during his handful of beef jerky, he began to happily chat once again. He talked about his journey, as a child wandering through much of this bush and the vast wasteland of the Sahara Desert. He talked of not finding food or water for many days as he walked with other lost children. He told me that he didn't understand why the world called them "Lost Boys" for there were many lost girls among them as well.

It struck me that only those who drank deeply from the cup of suffering could talk about the really hard things in life as the normal rhythm of it. Those of us who merely sipped from it seemed to wallow in self-pity.

As I ate my jerky and drank my water, I knew the biggest reason for my anger was that my spoiled life in America had taught me that I was not supposed to suffer. I wasn't supposed to have a sore back, a dry mouth, or an empty belly.

At home, if something hurt, I took a pill. At home, I had so many concoctions for my pain, so many cushions for the sharp edges of life that over time I began to believe I was entitled to be comfortable, exempt from suffering of any kind. At home, pain was something to be eradicated, not endured and taught by.

But I was no longer at home. And there were no pain pills for my back, no soft cushions for my seat.

Colliding Worlds

If I had paid more attention to "the little things" that James had been sharing with me in his weekly phone calls throughout the past year, I would have been better prepared for these sorts of miscommunications and misunderstandings.

In those calls, first he would give me the facts of how the ministry was developing, where our funds were being used, and how the children were doing. Then, I would ask him questions about his life and the community.

One day James told me that the general violence in the community seemed to be heating up. He said some migratory Arabs had raped a little five-year-old girl to death, not far from our orphanage.

In the same report he also told me, "A local man killed a woman last week. And she wasn't even his wife!"

Wasn't even his wife? What did their marital status have to do with the killing of a woman?

The worlds in which James and I lived could not have been more disparate. Nor could the norms of our respective cultures have been more incomprehensible to each other's. This young, complicated, wounded former child soldier had lived in refugee camps in three different countries. He straddled several cultures, and yet had none that was exactly his. My heart went out to him. Slowly, through James's stories of growing up wild in the bush and hungry in refugee camps, I began to glimpse hidden pieces of his heart.

It scared me to face the many things I would have to change about myself and my way of thinking if I would truly be a missional partner in this cursed country. My fear was a good thing; it drove me to ask God for patience with my ignorance, mercy for my arrogance, and grace for courage and insight.

I prayed daily for patience, divine guidance, and most of all, humility, as I knew that no training had prepared me for the hard work of dying to self that lay ahead of me. I feared this would take an unreserved dependency upon God Almighty that I lacked.

I apologized again for my outburst and assured James that we were in this together, whatever the outcome. The first thing to challenge in myself would be my sense of entitlement, including assumptions that I shouldn't suffer or be afraid.

Full of fear and my back still paining me, I climbed back on the bike with much more humility. This time I prayed in earnest for James's guidance and endurance, rather than my discomfort, as he propelled us through the thorny bush searching for our dammed-up trucks.

Chapter 11

BOY OR MAN?

Committing to James we were "in this together whatever the outcome," for the moment, meant being lost deep in the thorny bush of Sudan where slave raiders and genocidal maniacs ran free. More than anything I felt naive and foolish because I was so ill-prepared for all that unfolded around me.

Absolutely everything was out of my control, but what I felt most ashamed of was my inability to control myself. Mainly, I felt shame for my outburst with James. It was fear—and my sense of entitlement—that drove me to blow up at James even though he was on the same bike, lost in the same bush, and potentially facing the same slave raiders as I was.

I had to keep reminding myself of why I was in Sudan and what really mattered.

I was lonely. I wondered how lonely Jesus had been when He tried to talk with those around Him and no one really understood.

I was constantly hungry and thirsty. I wondered how Jesus found the strength not to turn the stones into bread.

I was afraid. I wondered how Jesus found the courage to willingly go to the cross when He could have called the angels to rescue Him.

When I dared to look closely at how Jesus spent His time on earth—and the fact that He called me to follow Him—I began to face the fact that most of what I'd been living for—comfort, status, even good things like church buildings or who won the next presidential election—didn't really matter. The only life that mattered was one that beat from the same rhythm as His.

The only difference between James and me was that he had been in training for this wild ride his entire life. When he stood just eight or nine years old, his village was attacked. In the chaos of the ambush, James took off running. He'd stopped expecting comfort, security, or even happiness a long time ago. He lived for a bigger, eternal purpose. I wanted that life, one that mattered.

He ran so long he found himself alone in the bush miles away from his family. He believed that his entire family had been slaughtered in the attack and that he couldn't return home because the Arabs would still be there … waiting for him.

James walked alone in the bush, picking up tracks and finding other lost children. One by one, the trail of homeless walkers grew longer as lonely orphans and straggling adults joined their ranks.

James was the baby in his family, and he was used to staying close to his mother. He missed her. His legs cramped from too much walking, and he cried for her comfort. When he was hungry and tried to eat leaves from the trees—and couldn't make them go down because his throat was parched and blocked with fear—he cried again.

James overheard a new man among them tell an older boy, "We will have to walk more than a thousand miles to find safety in Ethiopia." When James heard this, he stopped walking. He sat on the side of the road, next to an even smaller child, refusing to take one more step.

He sat in the dirt taking pity on himself and crying—until he heard the pounding. Fast, hard-falling footsteps. Turning just in time to see the lion as it lunged for the nameless child huddled next to him, James stumbled in the dust until he found his feet.

Pulling himself up and running as fast as his feet would rise and fall, James could not outrun the terrifying amalgamation of the small boy's cry and the lion's roar.

From that day on, anytime James felt too tired to walk, he remembered the pounding footsteps of the lion and the too-tired boy taking rest on the side of the road.

Passing the months and miles of the journey, James grew from a little boy crying for his mother into a vigilant survivor. He no longer allowed himself to think about the loss of his family, his fear, or his pain; nor would he let anyone see those tender places. He built high walls around his heart, keeping memories inside and everyone around him outside.

Placing one foot in front of the other, James grew into the life of a man before he was ten years old. He pressed on toward the thousand miles to Ethiopia and beyond. This transformed into the same pressing that drove him as an adult to make his way back to his village and begin the work of saving the orphans who never made their way out to safety.

Many years of hard living had prepared James for this moment of being lost in the bush. In contrast, I was just beginning to let my feet rise and fall along the path we shared. I feared I would come completely undone in the course, if we made it out at all.

I knew I couldn't talk about these things with James. The world I came from was every bit as foreign to James as his was to me. It would be unrealistic to expect him to comprehend the shock his culture jolted through me.

Stuck Trucks

As thorns ripped through my scalp, I busied my mind with images of our orphans playing, laughing, eating, and sleeping in trees to avoid the hyenas. Their faces reminded me what was at stake.

I assured myself that I was not suffering anything that all of them had not, and that as yet, I had not suffered nearly as much. The self-talk kept me calm and focused until the winding trail of a river snaked ahead of us.

"Mama Kimberly! See, I told you! This river ahead of us, it means we are very close now! Now we will find our trucks!"

I was thrilled to see the river but was too afraid of disappointment to hope very much, so I remained silent. We skimmed along the river's edge for a mile or two before we saw a couple of large dark objects poking up out of the water.

Our trucks!

As soon as I could see these were in fact our trucks with our drivers standing around them—protecting them from looters, bandits, or soldiers—I jumped off the back of the bike. Before James even cut the motor, I ran straight into the water. A few steps in, the spongy bottom snared my feet and landed my face flat in it.

I didn't care. I got up, pushed my muddy hair out of my face, pulled my wet blouse from my body to stop it from clinging, and continued my charge. James had chosen our drivers from Nairobi, so I'd never met them. Still they ran for me. How hard could it have been to pick out the one and only crazy white woman running out from the bush?

Munene spoke for them all: "Mama Kimberly! I can't believe you and James ... you made it! Praise God you made it! You came after us, and now you have saved our lives! Thank you, Mama, thank you!"

By the time I reached Munene, James's long legs caught up with me. Watching the two men hug and pat each other's backs, I remembered how afraid I had been, and how—while in the thick of the bush—I'd wanted to quit.

Now, just over an hour later, I stood in feculent water up to my knees being thanked for saving valiant men's lives. I'd never felt more joy or pride in my life! I was beginning to get glimpses of the joy that came from letting go, laying down my life, living from a bigger heart, and risking everything else.

James and I anchored ourselves in the mud by leaning against the current. We took care of our drivers first, doling out money for their food. They sent two men off to walk the few miles to the nearest market where they were to buy their first food in days. The others remained behind to guard our trucks.

We tried to figure out if there was anything else we could do to set our trucks free that hadn't already been tried a thousand times. Finally, realizing we were too tired to think productively, we decided we'd find a place to camp for the night and meet at the water's edge first thing in the morning.

The Weight of Darkness

James and I headed to a local NGO (nongovernmental organization) where we hoped to make camp. The first thing I noticed about the compound was that it boasted the same kind of security fence we previously had in Nyamlel: a dried-grass fence leaning ridiculously this way and that.

When women first weave these fences, the grass is still green. Over time the grass dries, and the fence turns a beautiful golden color, before it eventually fades into dead brown.

When planes fly low over the golden fences, the force of the propellers sways them like yellow lilies in a breezy field. From the ground, they provide about as much security.

Exhausted, I crawled into my tent and collapsed fully clothed—all the way down to my boots—without food, water, or a pit stop at the latrine. As I drifted off to sleep, I thanked God for allowing me to be a part of something so near to His heart and for leading us safely to the trucks. I also admitted I felt as stuck in my fear as our trucks were in the squalid mud. Falling into sleep, I dreamed.

My tongue was as dry and thick as a salt block. My face blistered from the boiling sun. Breaches erupted through the thin skin of my lips. Blood dripped from my head—although I couldn't remember why—and matted my hair to my scalp.

I wanted to cry out for help, but no voice would rise from me. No ear was close by to hear. No arm in reach to save or console.

From the dark desert silence rose a great thunder. I smiled, hoping maybe it was God coming for me after all. Lifting my head and squaring my shoulders in a rise of trust, I saw the "god" who would come for me.

The Janjaweed.

Before I could even turn, one of them on a swift horse swooped me up and over his legs, throwing me facedown, and galloping me hard toward my fate.

My fate.

Where could I go from here? I knew there was but one fate of utter darkness for me.

For me. The one who longed to be God's chosen, had been chosen by another.

By the only force in this forsaken land, I would be carried away to my fate.

The only one who came after me carried me to the place that had been prepared for me.

A perfectly squared, deep grave in the desert darkness.

There I was thrown.

There I was covered with mounds of sand until I could no longer hear my captor's howls of laughter, or his charismatic gunfire.

The weight of sand.

It threatened to crush my chest.

With great effort my breast rose and fell. Gasping in. Huffing out.

At my last breath.

A sudden pierce.

A reed forced through the sand, tunneling life-saving oxygen to me.

I knew this tomb was now my home, my fate, my passport to darkness.

I awakened momentarily paralyzed and drenched in sweat. Disoriented, my mind scrambled to get my bearings and remember where I was. Little by little it all came back to me. The trucks. Our drivers. And the reason for both, our orphans.

Raising my upper body, I slowly slid my feet off my cot to the desert floor. I had no watch, but I could see the sky through the mesh ceiling of my tent. The low-hanging full moon told me it would soon be outshone by the sun.

My tongue felt thick and pasty as in my dream. I rose to find water.

As I stumbled around the camp looking for a well or a holding tank, I kept thinking about my fearful outburst yesterday and my dream. I kept thinking I should be more together. I was a forty-something-year-old kawaidja mom whose children now were beginning to give her grandchildren, and yet the madness around me made me feel as though I were sliding off the edge of reason. I wondered how in the world a crying little boy who had suffered so much could grow into a larger-than-life man like James Lual Atak.

Looking for food and water—comforts James hadn't had as a child in the bush—I wondered what kind of dreams James had. Day by day, night by night, I was growing more accustomed to an array of emotions and facts of life that I had always tried to avoid.

Fear, loss, suffering, pain, anger were daily norms for James and all our orphans, as well as the 90 percent of the world's population that the wealthy Western world did not number among its own.

Something within me began to consider that maybe my fear and pain were the best gifts I could have been given. Something told me if I would stop running from them, I just might be transformed. But into what I didn't know.

I'd seen our orphans suffer without complaint as they endured fevers, cuts, hunger, death of family members, and many other things. I wondered if that was why Jesus said we must become like children if we are to enter the Kingdom of Heaven. They accept whatever is offered them and learn from it.

As big a man as James Lual Atak was, I began to think of him as the kind of child I wanted to grow up to be.

Chapter 12

THE COST OF A BATH

Slight rays of the sun struggling to rise above the edge of the earth offered my eyes scarcely enough light to make out a structure fifty or so feet dead ahead of me. Drawing closer, I cast the beam of my flashlight around its edges. It was a large canvas tent.

Lifting a loose canvas flap with my right hand, my left guided the beam around the dark interior. A covey of rats scurried off a rough-hewn table. Rats meant food was nearby. I hoped it meant sugar, because sugar probably meant coffee.

Trusting no vermin would want to be in the spotlight, I threw a shaft of light from wall to wall inside the tent. I draped and tied the canvas flap back, allowing the slowly dawning rays of morning to enter the tent with me.

At the rat's table I found a metal water filter. I righted a cup that lay on its side—where the vermin could lick out its contents—placed it under the filter's spigot, and lifted the lever. Empty.

Next to the empty filter, in a litter of spilled sugar and coffee crystals, sat a tin of instant coffee. I pried off its lid. Moisture had gotten into the tin, clumping the crystals into small rocklike formations. I dumped a hardened nugget of crystals into my hand.

At first I licked the crystal rock like a cow at her salt block. Impatient, I bit off a chunk and let the juices it puckered up in my mouth break it down until it was soft enough to chew. Bitter medicine, but medicine nonetheless.

I was so focused on my morning coffee, I startled when something touched my arm. Raising my head, I found a thin, dark-haired man standing next to me, studying me. Caught filthy in yesterday's dirt-caked clothes, stuffing my mouth with handfuls of coffee rocks, I flushed with embarrassment.

Involuntarily, my hand went to my head. It was a nest of hair, congealed with briars and blood. The man stretched out his hand offering me his water bottle.

I held his eyes just long enough to make sure I got him straight. Then I snatched the bottle from his hand. Without thanking him, I put it to my cracked and bloody lips washing down the gravel the coffee rocks had left behind.

My head buzzed and seemed to float above my body like a helium balloon. I tried to force myself to think clearly, but I couldn't focus.

As if listening through a funnel, I heard the man say, "The women deliver water just after sunup; more will be here soon."

I wanted to thank him for his kindness, but I couldn't find my voice.

He went on, "I am a doctor from Paris. I'm here trying to assess the actual impact of specific diseases in this hellhole. I hope to bring in vaccines for the diseases that we can identify; most we can't. This is a hard place. It will kill you if you let it."

Malek's Story

The doctor pulled two plastic chairs close to the rat's table. I dropped into one of them. He sat across from me, talking.

I couldn't move anyway so I listened as the doctor filled my buzzing head with one story after another. I can't remember much of what he spoke, but one story stuck in my head. It was about a local man named Malek who worked for the doctor. Malek could never leave the camp.

Malek received many death threats for working in the NGO camp. The locals were jealous because there were very few paid positions available, and everyone was starving. Everyone looked for any nugget of food, or the means to buy it.

While Malek was at work, villagers attacked his family. They looted what little food and blankets he had, then burned his home to the ground. Malek did not know if his wife and children had been able to escape. He didn't know if they were alive, and if so, where they were or how they were surviving. He was in agony and desperately wanted to find them.

The French doctor restrained Malek and convinced him it was too late. If he left the compound, he would surely be killed, and of no use to any surviving members of his family. Malek waited for the right time to go searching for his family. In the meantime he worked and gave thanks for his job that had cost him so much. He hoped one day it would provide for his family once again.

As my head began to clear, two women entered with large plastic containers brimming with water balanced atop their heads. In tandem, the women hoisted their jugs high into the air and then, in a graceful dancelike motion, lowered them to the lip of the metal water filters where they emptied them.

The muddy water filled our tent with the musty scent of the river. The smell reminded me of our trucks and the hard day's work of freeing them that lay ahead of us.

I felt tired and weak. I had one rough day yesterday. How could these women spend their entire lives this way?

I examined the rippling triceps in the arms of the water women as they hoisted their heavy cans of water. I considered how many times a day they would carry out this exercise. How many days in their lives would be spent pumping, hoisting, carrying, and pouring water for others? I marveled at how many times they risked rape and death by going out to collect water so that others might drink and live well.

I started to rise. The Frenchman put his hand gently to my wrist, directing me not to move. He refilled his water bottle for me one last time.

As I drained it once again, he moved toward a portable gas stove. Lighting it, he teased me a bit, "I really shouldn't give you a cup of coffee since you've already had several in solid form. But mercy moves me to indulge you with just one."

Thick as oil, it was the best cup of pure black coffee I had ever tasted. Life was beginning to pump inside me once again.

I turned to see men pouring into our mess hall. When I turned back around, my doctor friend was gone. I'd heard of mirages that our minds create for us in order to tender a measure of hope just when all seems lost—a bit of inspiration to keep us going. I wondered if he'd been a figment of my imagination. But then, I still had a hot cup of coffee in my hands. Perhaps he was my guardian angel.

The Cost of a Bath

Feeling stronger, I decided to brave the bathhouse, a mud-brick tukel where you could take a bucket of hand-drawn well water inside to bathe.

I was glad for the quarter-inch cracks in the wooden plank door because it let in shafts of light even when I closed it. Vigilantly eyeing a spider the size of my fist, I stripped.

First, I shook out my clothes. Still a bit intimidated at being the only woman at camp, I'd slept in everything down to my boots—just in case the need of a quick retreat arose. With a pool of dust flying from my clothes, I coughed, pushing out some of the particles I had inhaled.

I looked down at my brown legs and white feet. My legs were not tanned. Dirt from yesterday's wild ride colored them. My tightly laced boots kept my feet as white as the porcelain tub I wished I could soak in.

Having no washrag or soap, I plunged my hand into the bucket of already brown water. I lowered my face to hover just above the bucket where I swiftly raised handfuls of water to splash my face and neck.

I thrust my left arm into the bucket as deep as the bottom would allow—just shy of my elbow. Splashing, splashing. I switched to the right and followed the same ritual for my whole body, ending by standing in the bucket while drawing water up my legs and torso with quick dancing movements of my hands playing over my now trembling body.

The cool water stirred me. Surprised that this small pleasure reduced me to tears, I stood still with limbs outstretched and let the tears once again wet my face. The droplets evaporated in the dry desert heat before they could drip from my chin.

Dressing in the same clothes I donned the day before, I was relieved that the thorough shaking I gave them had at least rid them of some of their tenants, mainly sand. Unconsciously, my hands brushed against my hair. Ugh! The clots of dried blood and petrified mats of sand-filled hair tangled with small thorny twigs.

I finished dressing and stepped outside the bath tukel where I spied a large barrel of fresh water. I threw out my blackened water and plunged the bucket deep into the large barrel.

As if in prayer, I knelt beside the bucket and plunged my head in, hair tumbling in first. Head upside down, I let the water cover my eyes and reach the bridge of my nose.

Swish-swashing my head from side to side, I could feel the water making its way through my tangled mess and penetrating my ears. I pulled my head up out of the bucket and then quickly plunged it in again, covering my eyes once again several times, to free the dirt and blood.

The water turned close to the hue of my coffee. I stood, flipping my head upright, and enjoyed the cool water dripping down the back of my shirt.

The same water woman from the mess hall approached with a jerry can balanced atop her head. Watching her labor while cool, refreshing water dripped down my back evoked guilt for such an indulgent bath.

I'd seen her carry water for the men's evening meal the night before. I knew hers was the job to draw water for this huge barrel as well. She would have risen well before sunrise, walked to the camp in the dark, without aid of any light, save the same moon that I'd tossed under all night.

She would pump many gallons of water from a hand-pumped well in order to keep this barrel full today and every day, over and over again, day in and day out. There was no working her way up the corporate ladder or even the food chain. As long as she lived, this was as good as it gets. She would risk rape and her very life to find firewood in a largely deforested land in order to cook meals for the many men working in this camp.

Again, I glimpsed how those who suffer deeply seem to accept what is given them, learn from it, and forge a way to survive. So often I've thought of Africa and underdeveloped countries as primitive compared to ours.

The more I survived this wild country, the more I believed it was they who understood a higher calling and we who sank to primitive thinking, focused on ourselves. Our service, our giving, was conditional upon having excess. This woman gave service even when it meant risking her life. I'd poured most of what I'd had into building a certain comfortable lifestyle that stank with survival of the fittest.

Free at Last

As I walked back to the mess hall hoping to find James, all these things swirled in my head, chipping away at me, my assumptions, my values, and my way of looking at life.

James burst in the door moments behind me. Full of excitement, he bellowed, "Great news! God has freed one of our trucks! Our men started digging around their tires again this morning. One loosened quickly and now they are working on the second!"

I felt like crying again. Instead I said, "Praise God! Let's go to the river."

Long before we made the bend and could see our trucks, we could hear the men shouting and singing in celebration. Once we joined them, their joy was contagious. Watching them dance about,

I realized that while James had hired these men for wages, somewhere along the way the task had transformed them. It had swelled from a job to a mission.

I stood a few feet away watching the men dig out the second truck. Worn out from liberating the first one, Munene saddled up beside me.

As the second truck rocked back and forth seeking its footing to climb out of its hole, I glanced at Munene and saw tears streaming down his cheeks. He said, "Mama, in Kenya we think being a Christian means to go to church on Sunday and trying to be good through the week. Now I see it means suffering, being willing to let the hard things happen to you, so that God can use us to do His work on this earth!"

Munene's comprehension convicted me, and I joined him in tears. I knew if his insight bore truth for Kenyans, how much more for me and my people.

As the second truck rolled to freedom and pulled ashore, I dug through my backpack to find my camera. I wanted to photograph our heroic drivers with James, but Munene plucked it from my hands and gave it to a soldier. He pushed me to the center of our men, where I felt ill-deserving to be included among them, even for a photograph.

It's amazing what can happen to a person in twenty-four hours. Holding onto James as we returned to Nyamlel—to home—I felt thankful just to be a part of such a grand adventure, learning to accept whatever it brought.

Chapter 13

HOLDING THE
HANDS OF CHRIST

We made it home to Nyamlel in just six hours, not that I was counting. William and Peter gave us a welcoming home worthy of long-lost prodigals. I let James fill them in on our adventure. I laughed with them as he told the boys how afraid I had gotten, and then how angry.

"Mama's anger is a good thing, though! I tell you, when she is angry, she can really smash a lot of wild dogs' heads!"

As I pulled my cot next to Peter and William's tukel that night, Peter spoke through the cracks in the mud walls, "Mama, I am glad you are back. I know you can chase away anything that would hurt us."

I fell into a deep and dreamless sleep. In the morning, I did not wake before the sunrise as usual. A guard had to wake me. "Mama, they are here again. Many, many people have come to tell you their story."

The week before, we'd sent out word that I wanted to record testimonies of war, rape, persecution, or genocide. Anything anyone wanted to share, and wanted the world to know, I would hear. Hundreds of men, women, and children walked for days and piled around our gates, waiting to be heard.

The guard set me up in a tukel with a translator and two other witnesses. Here I listened hour after hour, day after day, learning life after life of the unspeakable things humans do to one another.

Knowing that African men do not normally talk with a woman beyond the necessary orders of the day, I was surprised to see how many men came to share their lives with me. Our guards told me it was because no one had ever cared to hear the horrors their families had suffered, and they wanted the world to know, even if it meant they had to talk with a woman. Tonj was among these men.

Eyes That Pierce

Tonj was a man you would easily pass by without taking much notice. He was not tall, not short, and slight of build, though not desperately thin. In his midforties, he kept his eyes downcast unless you caught and held them; then they were piercing.

This piercing first happened to me immediately after I noticed his right hand. It was not just that his thumb was missing, but from his index finger to his forearm was one smooth line. His outer palm and wrist bone were also gone.

By this time, I had heard so many stories of rape, torture, mutilation, and murder I was accustomed to staring into blank, nearly dead faces of the tellers. In some ways this made me very sad, like I wasn't reaching the people—getting to their truth. In another way, it helped me to get through the day; their emotional vacancy helped me to keep my own emotions somewhat at bay. So I raised my eyes from Tonj's thumbless hand, expecting to see those same blank "fish eyes." Instead I was met with liquid eyes of depth, harnessed power, and deep pain. I knew this would be a difficult interview.

Tonj never raised his voice much higher than a husky whisper during our entire time together. Humility and meekness sat before me, with his legs crossed, determined to tell the story of his wife and children. As the sole free survivor of his family, I watched this man struggle to represent them with dignity.

Facing me, I felt his cross-examination of my face, searching for sincerity. He would not prostitute his family by trusting their memory to someone he did not believe to be honorable.

Years before the attack upon his village, Tonj had stopped asking God for anything, save one daily prayer. "When the Janjaweed invade, please God, let me not be in the field or away from my family. Make sure that I'm at home and with them so that I can protect them."

God answered Tonj's prayer. When the day of the Janjaweed invasion came, Tonj was home. But he found there was nothing he could do except watch the violence unfold upon his family.

The Janjaweed rode swiftly on horseback, madly firing their machine guns and rifles upon men, women, and children of all ages. Above the screams and gunfire Tonj heard, *"Allah Akbar! Allah Akbar!"* ("Praise Allah! Praise Allah!")

The Janjaweed grabbed Tonj's neighbors and forced them inside their tukels. Setting the tukels on fire, the militia stood outside with guns ready to shoot should anyone attempt escape. The evil men laughed as children screamed in terror.

One mother fell dead from gunfire. Huddled protectively around his wife and five children, Tonj watched as a militiaman tore the dead woman's crying baby from the scarf securing him to her back. The evil man called to his friends to watch as he threw the baby on the roof of a flaming tukel. The baby fell through the brittle thatch where he died with his father and siblings.

Flames licked at Tonj's back as he tried to guide his family away from the violence. The chaos of smoke, screams, trampling horses, and gunfire wove a blanket of confusion around them.

Which way should they go? If they ran, he might lose one of his children.

Trying to form a plan, Tonj tightened the huddle he had around his family. He hoped to protect their hearts from the violence, as well as save their lives. Perhaps sensing Tonj's intense love for his family, more Janjaweed encircled him. They ripped him from his family's arms and pushed him to his knees.

While beating him with their pangas (machete), they yelled obscenities at him and called him an infidel. They demanded he call out, *"Allah Akbar!"* Tonj refused. He cried. He looked at his family, trying to say to them, "Be strong. Be still. Pray and wait." But only his eyes could speak.

Seeing the plea in his eyes for his family, several men charged at Tonj's face with the butts of their pangas, knocking out his front teeth. Finally, Tonj raised his hands over his head to shield himself. With his right hand crossed over his left, one of the Janjaweed pangas bore down on him, severing his thumb, outer palm, and wrist bone in one clean swipe.

Disgusted with Tonj's refusal to worship Allah, the Janjaweed kicked him over to his side. They left him there to bleed and watch as they turned their attention to his wife.

Seven men attacked Tonj's wife, ripping her from the protective huddle she struggled to hold around her young children. Tonj lay on the ground slowly bleeding to death. Helplessly, he watched these seven men beat and push his wife from man to man while laughing and calling Tonj an infidel and his wife a whore.

While the first man raped Tonj's wife, others kicked Tonj in his back and head. They laughed and yelled, "Now will you worship Allah?" Tonj cried out in agony—but no praise for Allah rose from his lips. All seven men raped and beat Tonj's wife while Tonj and his children watched in horror.

When they finished with her, they tied her hands together. Then they collected Tonj's children and bound them in the same fashion. Leaving Tonj for dead, they tied his wife and five children to the back of their horses and forced them to run behind as the army of Janjaweed rode north.

Tonj passed in and out of consciousness for some time; he was not sure how long he lay on the ground. The scars and missing body parts are more than symbols of his loss; they're a constant reminder. He has searched many times for any trace of his family, questioned every returning slave to learn if they have any word of them for him. Nothing.

The Nether Land of My Heart

I confessed to Tonj, "I fear I would not be as faithful as you have been. I am honored you would trust me with your family's story and humbled to sit with you. Please tell me, how did you manage to suffer such extreme persecution—and even more horrifying—witness the rape and torture of your wife and still not give into the Muslims' demand to worship Allah?"

With his steadfast and simple theology, Tonj replied, "Allah isn't God, so how could I worship him?"

Tonj told me that he'd never owned a Bible and could not read it if he had. He was introduced to Jesus through word of mouth and explained, "I know Jesus is the Son of God and that same Jesus died on the cross for me and my family. Why would I betray Him because of evil men?"

Mary Achai before surgery on her arms to repair the burn damage.

Woman wearing Kimberly's boots after trading her green flip-flops.

Orphans' school under mahogany trees as Kimberly first saw it.

James Lual Atak with one of the children.

Trees where children sleep to avoid being attacked by hyenas.

William Deng, Kimberly, and Peter Atak.

Kimberly resting from a motorbike ride.

Supply trucks stuck in the river.

Kimberly holding
Baby Elijah.

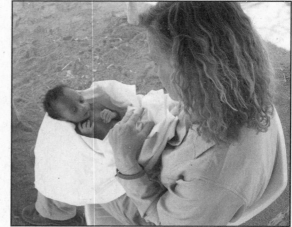

Dr. Jacoba "Conny"
Vrieling with child
at the clinic.

Little John on the side of the road looking for help.

James and Kimberly baptizing a woman in the river.

Kimberly blessing each child before she departs for the United States.

Sitting before this meek man of such unimaginable faithfulness, I had no words for him. I desperately wanted to comfort him as he cried for his family. I searched frantically for something. I had nothing to offer other than my presence, my witness, my heart. I gave all I had. I found myself wondering if everything else I'd ever given to everyone else prior to Tonj had been a lacking substitute for this kind of giving, coming empty-handed to make an offering from the nether land of my heart.

Clasping hands in our tears, Tonj's words pierced me, along with his eyes this time. "When I hold your hands, I feel as though I am holding the hands of Christ."

I held Tonj's hands and eyes until he seemed to say all he needed. Then, with no more words left to say, he stood with dignity, bowed slightly to me, and walked out the door.

I wasn't ready to move on. I wanted to spend time alone or talk with Milton. If he were with me, I knew he could help me make sense of this madness, or at least help me think of what to do about it. I felt lost and overwhelmed, but before I could even dry my tears, the guards brought in one more walking testimony.

I Am Tamar

This one was a mere child; she appeared to be all of thirteen. As images of what this beautiful young girl had probably endured flooded my head, I admitted to myself, I did not really want to hear from her. We'd positioned three chairs in the tukel; I sat in the middle with a translator to my right and the girl on my left.

"What is your name?" I asked, not really wanting to know.

"I am Tamar."

"Tamar, she was the daughter of David from the Bible," I said, sadly remembering how she was raped by her brother and never knew justice on this earth.

"What is your name?" she asked without looking at me.

"Kimberly," I replied.

"I mean your Christian name. What is your Christian name, your given name?"

"Kimberly *is* my name," is what I said, but what I thought was, *My God, will these people ever stop killing each other over the name that they chose or are given? "Christian: Peter," "Muslim: Mohammed," it's only a name. A name does not determine who you are or what you do.* Or so I thought at the time....

"Are you from Nyamlel?" I asked, trying to move on.

"I was born here, but they took me away a long time ago."

"They? Do you mean the Mujahideen? Were the Arabs alone?" Not wanting to look at me, Tamar reminded me of a large bird craning its neck to clean under its wing as she bent and twisted her head away from me, practically sticking it under her left arm.

I knew she meant the Muslims, but I'd heard—after forced conversions to Islam by the Arabs—the indigenous Sudanese from Darfur had raided along with the Mujahideen or Janjaweed too. I didn't want to put words in her mouth so I just asked Tamar to explain who comprised "they."

"Aye. *Nluck*." (This is a sound the Sudanese make by sticking their tongues to the roofs of their mouths and then sucking it off like a plunger being pried from a sink—the sound means yes.) "Darfur men came to take me along with the Arabs, but the Darfurees don't rape us anymore because the Arab Muslims have turned on Darfur.

Now the Arabs rape the women of Darfur and kill their men, just like they do to us."

"What do you mean, 'They don't rape with them anymore'?"

"When the Mujahideen got me, I was only this *agement* [she held her right hand to the side of our chair indicating the height of perhaps a seven-year-old]. Many of them got on top of me. I could not fight them off; they were so big.

"I tried to go to sleep, but I kept waking up as one would finish his angry work on me and the next would begin. I tried hard to sleep through them all, but I kept waking up, and another and another would be working hard on top of me."

"I am sorry." I wanted to express empathy but all I felt was nausea and rage so I dared not venture down that path too far.

"Did they mutilate you?"

Suddenly and without any preamble, Tamar lifted her legs to place her feet on the opposing arms of her white plastic chair as she brusquely raised her dress up to her chin. "Yes! See? They cut me here. I cannot feel anything down there anymore. Sometimes I just pee and pee and pee because I cannot feel when I need to go."

I fought against the storm of emotion that squalled against me. "Do you live with your family now?"

"No, they will not have me; I am marked. I bleed now, so I should be making babies for Sudan, but no man will have me because I am marked by the Mujahideen. I live in the bush. I heard that there was a kawaidja woman who wanted to know our stories. I wanted to talk to you. No one has ever wanted to hear what happened to me. We are not allowed to talk about it. Who will you tell?"

From what Tamar described, I knew she had suffered a fistula from the mass rapes. I also knew that if we had a sterile surgical unit, she could easily be healed for less than 150 U.S. dollars.

"Tamar, I will tell everyone who will listen. I will tell the world your story, and I pray that through your courage, the world will make the Mujahideen stop this evil."

"This would be a very good thing." Tamar pulled her dress down and stood to leave.

I wasn't ready for her to leave so quickly. "Would you like to take tea and biscuits with me?"

She smiled and sat next to me once again.

I got up to serve Tamar, but she jumped up from her seat. As an older white woman, it was unexpected for me to serve a young black girl. Gently as possible, I placed my hands on Tamar's shoulders and guided her to sit. I held her hands and eyes until she understood that I meant to serve her, as inadequate as I felt to do so.

As I drank my black coffee, Tamar drank hot tea with three heaping teaspoons of sugar and equal amounts of powdered milk and ate her English-style biscuits (sugar cookies). Neither of us talked, but we both learned more about each other through that silence than we had through all the words that had passed between us.

I sensed as rough and rowdy as Tamar came on, she was really a shy and gentle girl who had a hard time receiving my attention and care for her. Why should I expect her to trust me?

Ostracized at the outer limits of her village, no one was there for her. I listened to her and even cried with her, but in the end my empty hands were also empty for her.

I would send her back to bleed in the bush just as her family had, when—with a simple clinic—her chance at life could be restored.

When Tamar finished her tea and biscuits, she wiped her mouth with the hem of her skirt and walked out of the tukel without another word. I wanted to thank her, honor her, but the only thing my body knew to do was to stand for her as she walked out.

As soon as Tamar passed through the door, a dam broke within me. I fell against the mud tukel wall sobbing for the injustice, brutality, and utter darkness Tamar and so many others suffered.

I'd never known such evil existed, and—now that I did—I felt completely overwhelmed by it all. Useless against it all. I couldn't fathom what an appropriate response would be.

But there was no more time to be overwhelmed. The guards brought the next "Tamar" to me, and then another, and another, and then one more until finally, at sunset, James announced to the crowd piling around our gates, "That is enough for today. Mama is tired. You will have to come back tomorrow."

Chapter 14

REACHING OUT FOR HOME

James assessed my despair better than I did for myself. After clearing the people from our gate, he shooed everyone from the dining tukel and fixed me a strong cup of black coffee—just the way he knew I liked it. James drank his hot tea with mounds of sugar.

I studied James's face, amazed that he could serve me—the spoiled white woman—after having his heart scourged the whole day by the stories his people had suffered. Surely, I thought, the stories conjured his private memories of a thousand horrors from being a child soldier.

These were not just horrors from faceless crowds. They were the real life of his community, friends, and family. They were his reality too.

Our tukel grew dark, telling me the sun had disappeared from the end of the parched horizon. I could not see; but I heard the hollow clink of James's empty metal teacup as he placed it on the rough-hewn wooden table.

His arm brushed against me as he rose from his chair. Groping for my elbow, he gently encouraged me to my feet. "Mama, you are tired. Let me walk you to your bed where you can take a small bit of rest."

James walked protectively beside me as would a grown child with his aging mother. When we reached my cot, I sat on its edge wondering what to do next; I couldn't sort it out. James gently pushed my shoulders to the cot, raised my feet to the other end, and pulled off my boots.

His gentle acts of loving-kindness toward me—in the face of such atrocities he and his people had suffered—brought up sorrow within me from places I did not know existed.

A Lifeline to Home

I rolled to my stomach, turning my face toward the ground twelve inches from my cot. A dam of despair broke, flooding my heart with a tide of shame.

Despair for all those who shared their suffering with me; shame that I felt useless in the battle to help them. Like fire from heaven, too-long-held tears burned my eyes. Bile rose in my throat causing me to wretch, but my stomach had no food in it to throw up.

One part of me wanted to be left alone, push everyone and everything beautiful far away so that I could just free-fall into this pit of despair. Another part of me desperately wanted to be held, loved, comforted, and assured that everything would be all right. I wanted to respond to all I'd seen and heard, but I needed help to discern how.

Milton had always been that for me; and I for him. We'd traveled the globe together and had faced traffickers, pedophiles, murderers, oppressors, and many forms of evil. No matter in what dark bed we lay—as long as we were together—I always felt at home, or at least knew Milton was the compass that would direct us there.

Now my compass, my True North, pointed from some ten thousand miles away, and I lost sight of the needle. I felt rootless, plucked up, and cut off from my home, my navigator, and my nourishment.

It was difficult to keep my satellite phone charged on our small, constantly malfunctioning solar panel. So to conserve the battery for emergencies, most of the time I kept it powered off. I turned it on once a week or so to check in with Milton.

Those calls were precious to me, to hear my lover's voice, to hear about our children, and to share the joyful part of what I experienced with James and the women. I never wanted to spoil our brief calls by talking about the depth of fear, pain, sadness, and disorientation I felt.

Frantic, my mind tried to claw out of the pit of darkness I was falling into. How could I stop the madness and evil unfolding around me? How could I keep it from invading me?

I had no answers, and my tears wouldn't stop. As if from a long distance, I heard James asking me, "What is wrong, Mama? What happened? You were so strong all day, what is wrong with you now?" James sat on the edge of my cot where I lay crying.

Suddenly, I knew I could not do this alone. And, in that same moment, I also knew James was too close to me. Too moved by my tears. He reached to comfort me, touching my arm. I yelled at him to get away. "Leave me alone! I just need to cry! Leave me alone tonight; I'll be fine tomorrow."

I felt desperate for the comfort of another human, for strong arms to assure me all would be well. I knew that person needed to be none other than Milton, and especially not a young, single Sudanese man who had never had anyone to comfort him in his own suffering, until I came on the scene.

I tried to dry my face with the sleeve of my shirt, but more tears came faster than I could wipe away. I tried to assure James I would be okay. I explained I was tired and overwhelmed but after a good night's sleep, I would be fine. But my tears scared him; James was worried something horrible had happened to me.

No matter what I said, he'd experienced nothing in his life to prepare him for a woman in my state. It shook James to see me upset. Doing what came naturally, James reached out to hold me, comfort me. I jumped off the cot, reaching for my satellite phone.

I called Milton, and through tempestuous tears, explained as best as I could what was going on. I asked him, "Please explain to James that right now he needs to just leave me alone, let me cry like women sometimes need to do, and that I'll be all right in time."

With loving skill, Milton probed me with enough questions to know, in fact, I did just need to cry and was otherwise all right. Once satisfied, he told me to give the phone to James, who anxiously paced around me.

"Thank God, mzee! Kimberly is seriously upset. I think something very terrible has happened to her and she will not tell me what it is. I do not know what to do. I tell you, this is very serious. What am I to do?"

From there, James's end of the conversation went quiet for a long while with the exception of a few grunts of "Oh, I didn't know these things" sprinkled in here and there along the way.

By the time James and Milton's "Women 101" phone class ended, I'd cried myself to the point of starting to doze off. James dropped the phone at the end of my cot, and as if he'd gained all the worldly insight he needed to handle emotional women, he said, "You need a good night's sleep, so I will leave you to rest. But you know, Mama, your mzee is a very wise man! I wonder, how does he know women so very well? He knew exactly what to do with you from halfway around the world!"

Chapter 15

ELIJAH, CHILD OF HOPE

Early the next morning, open eyelids were the only indication I had that I was awake. The intense concentration I'd heard of senseless death and suffering coursed through my body as if it'd been pumped in with an IV. The oppressive concoction left my body feeling numb. I stumbled toward the latrine, anesthetized by the weight of pure and present evil.

I cried out to God wanting some sort of reconciliation of the ledger between life in Sudan and my life back in America, where relatively speaking, everything was so good. The stories I recorded daily were overwhelming just to hear. I couldn't even imagine living them. A part of me wanted to reduce them to something I could get my hands around, comprehend, and settle like an accountant with a neat list of numbers.

My mind rationalized that if I could just put the stories in some sort of ledger and find a sum total for them all, then perhaps I could find a purpose for the suffering. Then I might somehow make sense of it. I thought a purpose would make the suffering so much more bearable.

But there was no purpose. Pure evil lacks any intent, except utter destruction; and utter destruction makes no sense at all.

For many days to follow, a dark sense of profound futility bore down on me, and depression seemed to tug at me from all corners. With James's new insight into women's emotional lives, he let me be without too much prying.

At the end of most days, I still conceded to an evening walk. James chatted away telling unbelievable stories from growing up in the bush. Sometimes I'd draw close to my family by sharing tales of the antics my children pulled on Milton and me over the years.

Late one afternoon James and I passed through the dried-grass gates of the compound as we began our daily debriefing walk. Two women sitting on the ground next to the gate called out, "Mama Kimberly!"

One of them held a small wad of bloody rags in her arms, out-stretched to me.

As I turned and bent down toward her, she pulled back the rags, revealing a newborn baby covered in dried birth and fecal matter. James interpreted their words for me, but I didn't need anyone to explain the plea in their voice.

The rag-baby's mother had been attacked by a rabid dog. She survived the attack, but developed rabies. The trauma of it all brought on labor. She fought hard in a dank tukel for three days of labor. In the end, she died as she pushed forth new life.

Although these women knew the local folklore about a witch's curse for anyone who helped the newborn of a dead mother, one of them had been the best friend of the mother. She'd stayed at her side throughout her labor and death.

Knowing she was going to die, the young mother begged her friend to care for her baby. She begged until her friend promised the baby would live.

After the young mother died, the friend grew afraid and did not help the baby for several days. She left the baby to slowly starve to death in the same dark, dank tukel where his mother had died, without so much as cleaning the blood and the afterbirth from him. He was naked and alone.

Agonizing day and night, finally the friend remembered her promise. She had no means to care for the newborn herself, but she risked her life to bring the baby to us.

I held open my arms to receive the pile of rags cradling the crusty baby. His body burned with fever. I called for our cooks to bring me a bucket of water to bathe him. James rushed to the only market we had in the slim hope of finding a baby bottle and a nipple. Usually, about the only wares our market had were supplies stolen from USAID or UN food drops.

Cradling the baby's limp body in the nook of my right arm, I wrestled with a sheet in my left hand, trying to fold it in such a way to make a soft spot on the wooden table to lay the frail child upon. I smoothed over every wrinkle in the sheet, ensuring no bumps hurt his emaciated body.

As I bathed him, I gently searched his body for how it might direct me to care for him. If I pinched up a section of his skin between my fingers, then let loose, his skin remained in the puckered position. Dehydration had sucked out all its elasticity.

Our cooks gathered around, watching closely, but were too afraid to draw close to the child whose mother they feared called him to the grave. They were also afraid to get too close to me, for since I interfered, she may summon me along with the baby!

Somehow James succeeded in finding a dirty, scratched plastic bottle and a deteriorating nipple. As I cleaned the bottle, I remembered stories of Jewish prisoners dying when the Allied soldiers fed them too much, or the wrong food, too quickly.

I powered up my sat phone and called a friend for advice. Dr. Susan Ferguson Bradley walked me through the appropriate rehydration salts and water mixture. She told me signs of improvement to look for so I'd know when to introduce boiled goats' milk. She urged me to continue the baths for his fever. Susan cautioned me the baby's odds of survival were slim, but she was a great encourager for me to fight for his life with everything I had.

Raising a nipple full of Susan's concoction to the baby's mouth, I was surprised when he would not part his lips to receive it. I ran the nipple gently across his cheeks and lips, hoping to tease them open. No response. I used my pinky to pry his lips apart, gently slipping the nipple in place. Nothing.

The baby would not suck. I played the nipple from side to side in his mouth, again hoping he'd latch on. Nothing. He'd lost all will to live.

We had no IV fluids, and I knew every hour he went without nourishment carried him closer to death. Using an eyedropper from a vial of medicine, drop by drop I trickled life back into the precious child, defying the lure to his mother's grave.

After three days of eyedropper feedings, he latched on and tried to suck the dropper. Filled with a hope I hadn't felt in weeks, I brought the bottle back out. This time he latched on like a hungry lamb at its mother's teat.

I used one of the blankets VOM had sent us for distribution to concoct a homemade baby carrier, a sort of sling to tie around my body. Strapped to my torso, my papoose went everywhere I did. One morning while the baby was asleep in his sling, I began praying over him. The name Elijah came to me; I knew it was for him. Baby Elijah.

James felt it would be best if Baby Elijah could be reintegrated into his own culture. Once he was physically strong enough, James would find a close friend or family member who would raise the child.

When that day came, the friend of Baby Elijah's mother felt she should care for him, in honor of her friend. It seemed safe since, by that time, most of the village had moved on to other worries.

One day she came with another friend to collect Elijah. I'd grown to love him as my own but finally resigned myself to James's belief that it was better for him to be raised in his own culture by his own people. We agreed to make a place for him in our school when he grew old enough.

At the time, I had no way to foresee how costly the decision to let Baby Elijah go would prove to be, for all of us. Or, that out of it, I would make some of the most grievous mistakes of my life and cover my shame with a tarp of lies. The longer I held onto my shame—clinging to the lies I used to cover it—the more it felt like a dark secret that could never be exposed.

It was almost four years later before truth finally erupted through my cap of shame and fear, and not until I nearly bolted—almost walking out on my marriage, breaking my children's hearts, blowing up my life, and throwing away what God was doing in and through me. Nearly …

Chapter 16

ONE GOOD THING
LEADS TO ANOTHER

In the meantime, James and I grew closer, and he asked me to call him by his Dinka name, Lual Atak. Word of the Christians breaking local tradition and saving a baby's life spread like brush fire in dry-bush country.

Before Baby Elijah came to us, few people in the village knew who I was. Most just knew of rumors about a kawaidja woman in town who wanted to know people's testimonies, but for the most part I had met only those who came to share them with me.

As Baby Elijah's story spread, everywhere I went even strangers greeted me as "Mama Kimberly." Through his story, a great thing happened.

A few days after releasing Baby Elijah back into the community, James and I once again stepped through our grass gates for our evening bush talk. As we passed through, one of our guards asked me if I had ever met with the burned woman who came to see me.

"Burned woman? What are you talking about?"

Nervous now that maybe he would be in some sort of trouble, he looked at Lual Atak. "A woman named Mary came. She wanted to see Mama Kimberly. She was very seriously burned, but you told me make everyone wait their turn, and there were so many others who waited to see Mama."

Lual Atak couldn't quite control his irritation. "You must use your head, man! If the woman was seriously injured you don't just make her sit in the heat! Where is she now?"

"She lives in another village, across the river. I sent her home because I didn't know what else to do with her. She was not alone. Her son Matthew was with her. He was a big boy, already about ten years old."

It troubled me to know that someone in such a state had traveled so far to reach me and was turned away. James talked with the guard for a long time, making sure he understood to bring Mary to me straight away, if she returned.

The following day, as I drank my noontime coffee, I saw the guard proudly coming toward me. He looked as if he'd won the local fishing tournament; and his trophies, Mary and Matthew, inched along behind him.

Mary had indeed been severely burned. Months had passed since her escape from captivity and her burning, but the damage still ran so deep she could not bend her arms. Hardened scar tissue locked them in place, and fresh puckers broke open with each movement, oozing infectious puss and sending constant stabs of pain throughout her body. Her arms were stuck at a ninety-degree angle, unable to move up or down. Open places among the scars oozed a sticky fluid that drew flies and threatened further infection.

Her face bore thick open scars that ran down her neck and trailed down her back. The sun blistered her half-healed wounds. Once I directed her to sit, she took several moments to compose herself before apologizing, telling me that walking in the heat drained her last bit of energy, making even a short walk very painful.

Matthew was thin, but obviously Mary gave her son the majority of whatever food they scavenged, for she was gaunt. Matthew hovered over his mother with worry furrowed in his brow. I asked the guard to make them each a cup of strong tea with hordes of milk and sugar and to bring the whole tin of biscuits.

We sat in silence, studying one another until the guard returned. Then I let them take their tea before I asked any questions. Mary's voice rarely raised above a whisper. When neither I nor the guard could hear her, Matthew filled in the gaps.

Two days earlier, Matthew had been walking with his mother to help her find water. As two men passed them, Matthew heard them talking to each other.

One man pitied Mary. "Look at that poor woman. The Arabs! They have done this to her. They rape and torture our women and then leave them with nothing. If she was an Arab, they would help her. But because she is Dinka, they will do nothing for her. She should go to that kawaidja that works with Lual Atak."

The other agreed. "Yes. I heard they saved a baby in Nyamlel that was left for dead. Lual Atak and that kawaidja woman are Christians, and they will help anybody!"

But neither of them offered to help Mary themselves.

Matthew told his mother what he had heard. He begged her to ask the kawaidja and Lual Atak for help. After some resistance, because the walk would take nearly a whole day, Mary agreed. Matthew knew she would have to lean on him to make the long walk, but he felt hope for the first time in a long, long time.

Mary's wounds were so angry, her body so thin and frail, I couldn't see how she managed, even with Matthew's help. Matthew doted over his mother, picking at the blanket that was supposed to cover her wounds but was too small and rough to provide any real protection.

Mary never made eye contact. She stared intently at the ground or passed worried glances at Matthew. She did not immediately volunteer her story; I had to come at her delicately, slowly.

Matthew tried to speak for her; he told me she had six children.

She struck me as impossibly young to be the mother of six children. I directed my eyes and voice to Mary: "How old are you?"

I received the answer I was growing accustomed to but could never quite reconcile. "I can't remember."

Neither could she remember exactly when the Janjaweed had invaded her village. But Mary clearly remembered exactly where she was, what she was doing, and what the Janjaweed did to her and her children.

The chaos ignited by the fierce attack separated Mary and her husband. The children managed to cling to their mother. While Janjaweed looking not much older than boys set their home on fire, the select older members beat Mary and her children and tied them to the end of horses' tails.

As their entire village went up in flames, they were dragged deep into the dark desert night, to a fate only God and the Janjaweed knew.

Helplessly dragged along by the Janjaweed, Mary's feet cut deep troughs as they plowed through the sand. Stretching out before her, Mary's arms nearly jetted from their shoulder sockets, as if she were being pulled asunder on a torture rack. The rope's coarse hair burned through her wrists.

But it was the sight of her children trotting along beside her that pummeled a weight of darkness over her, threatening to press the very life out of her.

It was late into the night before they were finally able to stop for what Mary had hoped would be rest. Her hopes were soon stricken as the Muslim slave raiders secured the area by tying people down for the night and began dividing the women and girls among the Janjaweed. They raped young and old alike time and time again until the entire militia had their fill.

At morning's first light, the Janjaweed forced all captives to worship Allah. Mary refused. Enough of the captives did worship Allah that the Muslims did not seem too dissatisfied, for the time being. After "worship," the journey continued as it had the day before.

Time became a blur; Mary isn't sure how many days passed in the trek between her village and the town near Khartoum, where she was forced to "marry" her captor. She worked in the barn—where she slept—and became his domestic and sex slave. Mary's children kept their master's livestock.

In the beginning, Mary's captor daily tried to force her to worship Allah. She held her ground. He beat her, threatened her, and even threatened her children. Mary remained faithful to Christ.

Over time her captor became less interested in Mary and focused more on her children. Each day he sent them to a place where they were forced to learn of Allah and how to worship him. Out of fear, Mary's children followed the ways of their captor, and Allah.

Mary lived this life of humble servitude for many years and bore her captor several children. When Mary's oldest daughter grew to about ten years old, Mary's captor's original wife, an Arab-Muslim woman, told Mary their husband was going to sell the child to another slave master who wanted a young virgin sex slave.

Although Mary had suffered quietly, thinking of her daughter enduring the same violent rapes she knew so well sent her over the edge. Mary decided she—and her children—would be better off dead than for her daughter to endure life as a sex slave.

She decided it was worth the risk to attempt escape. With the aid of her master's original wife, Mary gathered all of her children, including the ones she bore through violent rapes.

In the middle of the night, while their captor slept, Mary and her children fled on foot. When her master awoke in the morning, he did not smell the fire warming his morning chai. He assumed Mary had overslept and stormed the barn to kick her awake.

When he saw the straw mats vacant, he knew Mary and her children had escaped. He set out on horseback to reclaim his "property."

Knowing she and the younger children would slow down the older children and reduce their chance to escape, Mary sent her three older children—boys old enough to run on their own—in one direction while she kept her nursing infant and toddler. Mary also kept her ten-year-old daughter with her.

Although they had a head start of several hours, her captor's horse caught up with them very quickly. When her "master" found her lying on the ground trying to hide in desert brush and protectively covering her children with her body, he circled her many times on his horse firing his gun in the air as he screamed, *"Allah Akbar!"* Mary was terrified and dared not move.

In the end, her former captor decided shooting them would allow them to die too quickly. He deemed a more fitting punishment for their escape was to burn them alive. He set the bush shielding Mary and her children on fire and rode off satisfied that he had killed her—slowly, with much suffering.

On fire herself, Mary struggled to drag her infant and toddler from the flames. Her infant died before she could get out. Mary crawled out of the flames, dragging her toddler behind. Drifting in and out of consciousness, Mary laid on the desert floor for several days.

Mary's ten-year-old daughter also died in the flames. Her toddler survived for some unknown hours, but at one point when Mary aroused from unconsciousness in extreme pain, she found her toddler dead beside her.

Mary's older sons, whom she had sent in the opposite direction, met up with a Dinka man. The man agreed to help the boys look for their mother. Together, they found Mary unconscious.

This Dinka man carried Mary back to his village and cleaned her wounds as best he could. Even with his help, without adequate medical care, her severe burns developed thick scar tissue around raw open wounds that continued to ooze and risk further infection.

After a few weeks of healing, the man helped Mary get to her home village where she looked for her husband. The news was not good. At first villagers told Mary that when she and her children were taken as slaves, her husband set off into the desert looking for them, and he was never seen or heard from again. She didn't know if he died en route or was captured himself.

In time, sadly, she learned he was alive. He just didn't want to be with her because he'd heard she was ugly with scars and couldn't even collect water due to her burns. Besides, he'd married another woman.

A Better Life and a Livelihood, Too

When Mary first came to James and me, she was at great risk of dying from starvation, if infection didn't get her first. In Sudan, the only hope for a woman's survival and protection is to marry. But her husband wouldn't take her back, and no other Sudanese man would marry a woman in Mary's condition. Her wounds rendered her unable to pump well water, collect firewood, or cook—the only things the culture considers a woman has to offer besides sex and childbirth.

We did all we could to comfort Mary, but I knew it was not enough. Our medical clinic had no sterile surgical unit, and the surgery she required was complicated. My friend Lisa Thompson, human-trafficking liaison with the Salvation Army, called the U.S. State Department on our behalf, hoping to get a medical visa for Mary. She was told it was not possible to help the Sudanese women due to bad relations with the Sudanese government.

I called Dr. Dick Bransford, a missionary friend in Kenya. If we could get Mary out of Sudan, he agreed to perform surgery on her in an attempt to restore her arm movement. Voice of the Martyrs arranged to pay her bill, and Africa Inland Mission (AIM) flew her to Kenya. Dr. Bransford was able to restore 90 percent mobility in her arms!

I introduced Mary to a short-term mission team that came to work with us. Dwight Williams, a musician on the team, had a wonderful idea of a microenterprise for Mary. He asked if she would like to weave crosses from the kind of brush grass in which she had been burned. Mary was enthusiastic about it. Within a few days, she delivered hundreds of them to us to take home and sell for her. Mary was off and running with our first microenterprise!

The team gathered enough funds to build a tukel for Mary, and we enrolled her children in our school. One day I went to visit Mary in her new home. I was astounded to see she had moved other widows in to live with her. No one told her to, or even taught her to, but there she was being Jesus to others around her. She also shared her meager earnings from her microbusiness to feed other women who had suffered.

Mary had no training. She could not read or write and did not own a Bible. Yet, giving to others flowed naturally out of her from a Christ-like love. She asked me to begin a women's Bible study and help her to become a leader. Two other women came alongside her, Marydit and Teresa. Together, these three women lead a powerful women's ministry in a land where women are scourged and discounted.

God's Hand on Others Touched Me, Too

Reflecting on the journey to this point, from Tonj to Tamar to Elijah and Mary, with bouts of despair riddled between, I again found God's stones in the turbulent waters of life. New partnerships had formed, and I was ecstatic to see different parts of the body of Christ work together in partnership to do such a beautiful work. I started tracing back through the many ups and downs—dark and lonely times when I could make no sense of anything.

In the last few months, I'd suffered things that had intricately woven a golden thread of me into the tragic fabric of the Sudanese story, and I didn't feel ready to leave Mary, Baby Elijah, and many others I'd grown to love. I called Milton to express my doubts and pain about leaving. The call went badly, very badly.

I told Milton, "I feel if I go back to my comfortable life in the States I'll be abandoning countless women and children who cling desperately to the brink of hopelessness. I've had so much they've never had. A loving husband. A safe home for my children. Endless food and water. I just can't run home, leaving them in this despair."

Milton couldn't understand. He heard, "I love them more than I love you. I don't appreciate your love for me. You don't satisfy me. I'm going to be unfaithful, abandon you, and choose them over you."

Words bouncing off static-filled airwaves between satellites were never going to bridge the gulf hewn between Milton and me by the extreme things I'd been exposed to but did not quite know how to face or even admit yet. Nor would they assuage the anguish Milton carried daily as he longed to know his wife was safe and back in his protective arms.

As the team left, I reconciled myself to head out with them. It seemed like the only thing I could do, but it left my heart feeling small and squeezed out. I'd been gone more than three months. I wondered what waited for me at home, and if I could receive it.

Chapter 17

DANGLING AT THE
END OF MY ROPE

Being home was bittersweet. What waited for me was everything a woman could want, and everything the women I loved in Sudan didn't have. Over the following four years, I worked to find a balance between time in Sudan and time at home with Milton.

Up to this point, Milton and I had always relied heavily upon each other. This new life of spending so much time apart pushed both of us to cry out to God rather than reach for the other. In that way those years took us deeper into our own spiritual journeys. At the same time, a dangerous gap of silence was growing between us.

As I watched diabetes take its toll on Milton—combined with the fact that each time I left him for Sudan I experienced a shocking dimension of life and death for which he had no frame of reference— I hid more and more of the harder parts of my journey from him. Milton knew I had things bound within me that I either couldn't or wouldn't trust him with.

He rightly sensed they were so foreign, dark, and painful that I needed time. He wouldn't force, but he did probe. Each time I reacted as if he stuck me with an electric cattle prod, and I grew a little more silent.

I told myself, "I've made it this long. What good would it do to hurt him with the truth now? What right did I have to unload myself on him when I knew how it would grieve him?"

I tried to make up for my emotional distance by showing Milton love in physical ways. I fixed the special foods he loved, delivered unexpected cups of coffee, sought out and gave serendipitous gifts, and made concerted efforts to be less selfish in our sex life. Milton enjoyed the special attention but rarely ever let me forget it was *me* he wanted, not what I could give him or do for him. For the most part Milton was patient with me, trusting I'd talk when I was either ready or when life brought me to such a place that I couldn't bear it any longer.

My own pain festered as I feverishly lived a mission of mercy in Africa and Eastern Europe, alternately traveling the United States on a mission to mobilize the church through speaking tours, sharing the plight of the oppressed, persecuted, and trafficked. While I spoke on behalf of others' suffering, shame numbed my heart and fear froze my tongue for nearly four years while I begged God to help me see the way to my own freedom.

Groping for the Strength to Open Up

The big thaw began after dragging myself home from a meningitis outbreak in Sudan. I more closely resembled one of the corpses I left behind than the wife Milton expected to meet at baggage claim.

Gaunt, baggie-eyed, with my face so taut with tension it looked as if it were bound in shrink-wrap, I did the best I could to put on my game face for Milton. Still, he hesitated as I approached, looking uncertain whether he should sweep me up into his arms or call a paramedic. I looked better than I felt.

I made the decision for him by falling into his open arms while strangers filed by, gawking at the good-looking man clinging to the vagabond who stank up their plane. The time we spent waiting at baggage claim for my dirt-caked duffel bags is a blur. I do remember Milton lugging my bags from the conveyer belt and making me sit on them at the curb while he went to get the car. He said he doubted I could walk the negligible distance to the short-term parking lot.

Once loaded, I'm certain we spoke on the way home from the airport, but most of the trip is lost on me now. I only remember taking note of how smooth the ride was. There were no dried ruts in the road to maneuver, no dying babies lying in frail mothers' arms on the side of it, and no families carrying convulsing loved ones on homemade stretchers trying to get to our makeshift clinic.

As he turned into our driveway, Milton used his clicker to open the garage door. Out bounded our three rescue puppies clambering to see me and whining for me to love up on them. Snatching them from impending euthanasia as newborn pups, I'd loved and cared for them like babies. Now, as I let them lick my face and prance around me, my mind worked hard to remember that they would not tear my flesh from my bones or eat off my face like the wild dogs and hyenas do to orphans in the Sudan desert.

Quietly in my head, I talked myself down from a high tower of fear. "I'm home. I'm safe. I'm with my husband who loves me. My children love me and will visit soon. There is food inside my house—inside an electric refrigerator to keep it safe for me until I want it—whenever I want it. I am okay now." Or so I told myself. But the sadness and anger boiling inside didn't leave me feeling okay. I felt like I was dying.

Milton literally carried me up the stairs, drew a hot bath, and lowered my exhausted body into the soothing water. As the water swirled around me, he gently washed my body, scaling away dead skin with a loofah. Focusing on my hands, he worked a soft brush across my dirt-caked fingernails until the grit floated in the water around me. Moving to my feet, he pumiced the stains from my calloused heels.

Draining the filthy water, he ran more to lather my hair twice and rinse the grime away. I wished he could also wash away the hidden guilt and shame I felt—from failures I'd seen and committed—during the meningitis outbreak. Tears streamed down my clean face as I longed for every widow and orphan suffering alone in this world to know the same love Milton lavished on me in this moment.

Putting me to bed with a chunk of my favorite cheese and a glass of red wine at my bedside table, Milton filled me in on our children's lives while I ate silently. Clean and full for the first time in weeks, I folded myself into his arms. The last thing I remember of my first night home is Milton kissing my face, caressing my hips, and telling me everything was going to be all right.

When I awoke the next morning, it seemed Milton's words were prophetic. Everything did seem all right. I was happy to be home, and the first few passionate days of catching up with Milton—on everything from lovemaking to family matters to bill paying—sped by.

Too Much to Process

Slowly, as weeks turned into months, we began to settle back into our daily routines, and little things began to rob my joy. Milton would caress my arm, and the faces of young girls and old women alike who'd never known the touch of a man—except through rape—would crowd in around my warm feeling and squeeze the life from it.

Or our children would visit, and I'd find myself relishing in their antics from college or work. Just as quickly, though, my mind would turn to an orphan in the bush sleeping on top of her mother's grave. I would tell her, "I'm sorry, we do not have any more room in our orphanage. Soon I hope we can build more," all the while knowing "soon" would not be soon enough for her.

Sometimes I'd be eating dinner or in a meeting or on the phone with a donor when sudden despair would overtake me. All I could do was weep, or at times just walk out.

Life began to close in around me. I told myself to just keep going, and in time, things would get better. I'd feel better. Life would go on. But I was beginning not to believe my own hype, and all I wanted to do was run away.

Having always been the emotional conduit and barometer of our marriage, my silence created a tension we'd not known before. Milton was left to figure out what was going on with his wife.

"What's happened to you? What aren't you telling me? You always talk about the importance of intimacy, sharing, and time together, but I feel you're hiding from me … you're talking to me, but you're not telling me anything. Each time you go to Sudan, less of you returns home to me."

I stonewalled, trying to buy time. I kept turning things over in my head again and again, this way and that, trying to figure out how to get through this impasse without admitting the dark secrets that kept mounting within me. I knew my secrets were splitting my marriage right down the middle; but I'd dug a black hole with them, and I just couldn't seem to find my way out. Hiding does that between couples, even if the hiding seems to have what we consider a worthy goal.

Milton saw—felt—me contemplating. But I kept up the barriers and wouldn't let him in until one sweltering summer night when just the right brick shifted to topple the wall.

Complaints, Caterwauls, and Confessions

It was a rare weekend when Milton and I had neither work nor family commitments. We spent all day Saturday swimming in the lake, reading, and talking about the books we were reading, or just talking about nothing at all.

By sunset we were both tired. We climbed the nearly one hundred stairs from the lake to our back porch, flopping into premier seats for the sun's final display of red strokes. As darkness settled in around us, some little something passed between us in just the right way to spark an argument. I was the first to pick up the mantle—but with months of tension egging us on—within moments we were both going at it.

We pushed back and forth with unoriginal fodder. "You always" and "you never" seemed to be our chief complaints of the evening. On my feet and at the ready now, we were on the fast track for the kind of caterwaul most good families deny ever takes place within theirs ... when Milton suddenly broke into laughter. "This has been a perfect day. We've had fun together. I've loved watching you dive, swim, or just lay around seducing me in your bathing suit!"

As I stood over him, from his wicker rocker Milton grabbed

me around the small of my waist, his eyes tugging at my heart as he continued, "What in the world are we fighting about, really?"

My tears broke like summer's clandestine thunderstorms, as my words thundered at him.

"We're fighting because I'm absolutely livid! We're fighting because I have a good and loving husband who loves me enough to hang in there when I am absolutely impossible. Who I know would lay down his life for me, who stands up and fights me, or chases me when he knows I'm running, or reaches down and pulls me out from between the rocks when he knows I'm hiding from him. We're fighting because I have all of that, and I can't even save one little child bride who desperately needed me to fight for her. I failed her. I couldn't even be there for one. I feel like such a lying hypocrite I can't even stand to look at my face in the mirror; I can't imagine why you want to see me nearly naked in my bathing suit!"

The thunder draining out of me, I dropped from his hold and melted into a puddle of sobs on the porch. Milton gently put his hand out to me, as he has done thousands of times spanning more than twenty years.

Pulling me up into his lap, he whispered, "What are you talking about? What little child bride? Kimberly, there is nothing you can tell me that will make me run away from you."

Whimpering now, "I'm not afraid of running you off. You're so faithful; I know you'll stay. I'm the unfaithful one, and I'm afraid I won't be able to bear you looking at me with such love and forgiveness. I'm scared *I'll* run away."

"Kimberly, trust me. Talk to me."

So, I did. I told him the story I had never told anyone. For the

first time, I took my husband to Sudan—back to the meningitis outbreak—and my haunting memory of a young girl named Elisabeth,
from where my heart had never returned.

*Dead asleep, I sprang alert when one of our guards, John,
shouted, "Mama Kimberly! Mama Kimberly! There's another
one, come quickly!"*

*My first urge was to yell at John, telling him to go fetch
James first. Then my heart sank. I remembered James had hurt
his back from lifting too many sick, dying, or dead bodies. I
had given him pain pills and put him to bed; he was down
for the count.*

*Before climbing out of my too-small tent or even respond-
ing to John, I cried out to God, "What am I to do? What else
do You want from me? What can possibly be different this
time? Why should I even bother to go just to watch one more
person die? I am sick of being an usher for death! Where is the
hope You promised?"*

*As I rolled over, I heard my clothes crinkle from the baked-
on blood of those who'd already died against my desperate fight
to save them. I bent down to lace up the thorn-scarred boots
still cladding my feet.*

*Outside I picked up on John's breathless pant: "There's a
man at our gate. He says his niece is too small and she cannot
push out the baby lodged inside her. They are scared because
she now has the meningitis. What can we do?"*

*I knew, and wanted to shout out the terrible truth once and
for all, "Precious little. So go away and don't wake me again."*

Instead I said, "I'll get the truck."

Jumping in the open back, John gave the roof a proper pounding, signaling me to grind the gears into action. Roaring up to the guard shack, I swerved to miss the pile of sleeping bodies who waited for daybreak to be the first in line when our clinic reopened.

In my zealous overcorrection, I nearly ran over the waiting uncle. Once in the cab with me, we both breathed a sigh of relief, even as our stomachs churned to be on our way to where we knew death burned at the edges of life.

The uncle's sparse English and my limited Dinka relegated us to hand signals and grunts. I knew to go this way or that by the directional thrusts of his hands.

He smelled of death. His odor raised a flood of memories from my first visit to Sudan. Back then, I was ill-prepared for the smell of people who were filled with disease and parasites, left without sanitation, and had no food and little water. What water they did have was putrid and full of animal and human feces alike.

When crowds pushed in around me, the smell scared me far more than the mob. In the early days, powerful urges to run would threaten to drive me farther into the wilderness where I hoped no one would find me.

If I ran, I wouldn't want to be found by the Sudanese, for they begged me to save them, and I was utterly powerless to do so. I wouldn't want to be found by other Americans, for I feared judgment and would bear great shame for my cowardliness to have run.

Now I sit behind the wheel of a banged-up Land Cruiser driving toward certain death, with its scent as my sidekick. All I can think is, Fine. I'll go, but I already know what is going to happen. It's pointless. I despise the waste of it all. I feel like human waste.

In the long-forgotten rainy season, trucks had spun deep in the mud, creating small ponds where villagers collected their daily drinking water.

Lately, dry season had fallen hard upon us, leaving mummified arroyos of hardened ruts and holes we called roads.

As both my fists clutched the wheel, the constant jostling hurt my back but also provided protection from the hard work of conversing with the worrisome uncle.

Trees are sparse at the cusp of the Sahara Desert. When you unexpectedly come upon one, the barrenness strikingly frames the beauty as a tall, dark mahogany looms over rutted roads and undergrowth.

As we plowed through the brushwood to reach the young laboring girl, whom I learned went by the Christian name of Elisabeth, branches of mahogany swept against our windshield, cleaning a layer of smut from the glass.

Tears rolled down my cheeks as I anticipated the next few hours. I prayed, "Oh, if only You would send mahogany branches to wash away the tears of this family, this people."

Without a word from the uncle, I knew we were drawing close to Elisabeth. Gripping the black plastic balance bar drilled into the dashboard just above the glove box, the uncle pushed his face near the windshield, straining through the dark to see what appeared to be a cluster of tukels. I slowed, but the uncle stayed at the edge of his seat.

That's when I first heard them—the screams. I knew what they meant. I knew I did not want to get any closer to them than I was in that moment.

I choked and bottled my fear, but I was no less panicked than the screaming Sudanese.

A rush of terror flushed me as I considered what I was about to face with no knowledge or training of how to face it. In spite of my fear, I felt something stronger beckoning me to go. Pulling me toward Elisabeth.

I had run from pain and fear most of my life. I was still afraid, but I had finally reached a place where a larger part of me wanted to draw near to that quiet but compelling voice that asked me to trust in something outside of myself.

I knew that voice was God, but I doubted Him. From where I sat, He seemed to be losing a whole lot more than winning, and that scared me. I wanted to trust. I prayed for a scrap of faith. I doubted.

As we climbed out of the truck-turned-ambulance, women were already grieving in the way that always turns my stomach in knots to witness. They jumped high into the air and threw themselves harshly to the ground, often bashing their heads on the rocky soil.

Their vocal cords pushed out something indefinable—not quite cries, shouts, or screams, but something surely of the agony you would hear in hell. They call it ululate, and this wailing is sometimes used to mourn, sometimes to chase death away—perhaps to another compound down the furrowed road.

Again, I cried out to God, "For all our sakes, this time— please—use their screams to chase death away from this house."

Panic had overtaken the villages as day after day more families were struck down by meningitis. In Sudan, when a meningitis outbreak runs amok with no vaccines, you watch the living for signs of the deadly, contagious disease. Each person vigilantly watches his neighbor, brother, sister—everyone.

When I saw the signs in a child, I wish I hadn't been looking.

Elisabeth had been in labor for two days. No one panicked about this fact. In Sudan, it's common for twelve- and thirteen-year-olds to be raped or given in marriage, become pregnant, and die in childbirth before they are even ready to leave home, where they help their mothers cook and listen to their fathers tell stories long into the dark of night.

Men rushed in around me. I felt faint. They ferried the smell of death that stabbed and gathered up at the back of my throat, gagging me. One man grabbed me by the arm. In that moment I realized it wasn't just my fear gnawing at me. I had been absorbed and carried by the mass hysteria of all the people trapped in the meningitis outbreak.

The man who gripped my arm pushed me along through the crowd to the tukel I knew sheltered Elisabeth. Thrusting me through a blanket draped between the mud-brick doorframe just beneath the straw roof, I groped blindly in the dark for the next person I knew would seize me, forcefully guiding me to Elisabeth.

Bumping against heads and shoulders, my eyes began to adjust enough to make out the sketchy lines and features of my fellow medical team. I have zero medical training, yet they shoved me to the front lines of Elisabeth's war against death.

Under normal conditions, as a foreigner I would never be asked to assist in a delivery. Most Sudanese women are highly adept in attending new life brought forth at the brink of death. However, as the only mzungu (another local word for wealthy white person—I was wealthy because I was the only person with a meningitis vaccination), I had become a wildly sought-after commodity.

Meningitis is so contagious that even the vaccine is only about 70 percent effective. Still, my odds were certainly better than the locals'. Most nurses had bailed out weeks ago. A combination of fear and lack of wages for the preceding six months drove them away.

Straining to see the sketchy outlines of bodies inside the dark, smoke-filled tukel, I fell to my knees. While my eyes worked overtime, all my other senses begged to shut down.

My skin crawled over my bones as it adjusted from the cool desert night air to the heat inside the small dank tukel stuffed with too many bodies and filled with the pungent odor of blood, earth, urine, and straw.

The low cook-fire built in the dirt floor of the tukel filled the small hut with smoke. My eyes puckered and watered. As the smoke made my nose run, salty drippings ran into my mouth. My ears stung and tried to shut out the screaming sounds of impending death coming out of twelve-year-old Elisabeth.

As my feet bumped into something in the dark, I fell to the ground fingering around for Elisabeth. I found her knees first.

Lying flat on her back with knees jutted into the air, Elisabeth's feet used the earth as leverage to push her back off the floor as she writhed in pain, groaning to expel the too-large baby trapped inside her underdeveloped body.

More screams came from her fearful, panic-stricken mother, aunts, and uncles, all demanding I do something to save both lives.

I played my hands across Elisabeth's belly trying to learn her size and the baby's position. A pale beam streamed across her small body from above my head. Someone had a torch, a flashlight. I praised God for small favors as I continued to search Elisabeth's body for clues it would offer me as to how I could help usher in new life.

Again I pleaded with God, "What do You want from me? What would You have me do?"

I determined that Elisabeth's family was right. Her violent convulsing was not simply labor; we had all seen it too many times these last few weeks. Elisabeth's body arched from meningitis.

Her belly was like a rock in a fire pit—hot and ready to explode. If the shouts and screams in the room were bees, the room would have been so full that you would have swallowed ten of them every time you opened your mouth. Stinging you slowly to death from the inside out.

I shouted above the buzz. "Elisabeth, my hands feel your contractions. The baby wants to come out. Can you push?"

No answer. Just more screams as I felt the contractions press hard on her belly. My hands pressed downward from high on Elisabeth's abdomen attempting to help the contractions do their bidding of birthing a baby while saving a young mother's life.

My hands drifted down the hard mound of her belly, seeking evidence of new life from the wet cave between her legs.

Blood! "My God! That is blood! Elisabeth, you are losing a lot of blood!"

The pale beam raced across the dirt floor as it thirstily swallowed up her blood. This is what the family had been trying to tell me. Elisabeth couldn't hold out much longer.

Now that I knew what our communication barrier had prevented me from understanding earlier, the family's screams became much more insistent—directional.

"Do something! Save her! Save my little girl. Save my child bride. Save my baby! Do anything—but save her, mzungu!"

Of course, these Dinka-speaking tukel dwellers did not say those harsh English words to me. But I swear that is what my broken heart heard.

Elisabeth screamed in pain. Her family yelled in fear and panic. I felt her belly grow harder with contractions that had gone on for two days without yielding results.

I shouted, "Push! Elisabeth, please help me! Push!"

Nothing more from Elisabeth.

Again, I cried, "Please, Elisabeth. Help me. You've got to push!"

Still nothing.

I couldn't remember the last time I had water to wash my hands. I ran out of gloves many days ago. Still, I knew that baby had to come out.

As if having minds of their own, I felt my hands dig deep into the tight cave of Elisabeth's too-small body, hoping to get a grip around her baby and pull.

Gently but quickly they found the baby's head and a small shoulder but could nettle no farther. My mind didn't know what to do with the information my hands were uploading. My hands had gotten themselves into this mess and would have to figure out what to do on their own.

My fingers fidgeted about until they found a place where they thought they could do a bit of pulling, when suddenly Elisabeth arched one last time. A final time.

Elisabeth's screams stopped.

The family's wails quickened.

With my hands still inside the small one splayed before me, my mind began registering what just took place. I struggled to process what had happened. My hands lingered—not wanting to give up the fight.

Elisabeth's knees went limp and fell slightly outward, expelling my hands from within her. They were covered in blood and other matter, but they brought forth no baby.

I raised my empty hands to my face, screaming into them as if they could catch my grief and carry it far away. They failed.

Joining, at least for a time, Elisabeth's family in the senseless, futile, hopeless battle against death in a land of government-sanctioned genocide, persecution, torture, rape, and slavery, I forgot I was an American with a blue passport. For a moment, I forgot I was white, or that Elisabeth was black.

For a time, I numbered among the suffering, for I agonized with them. For a time, I was just a broken child of God, disoriented and overwhelmed by how cruel this world can be.

I did not know how healing and meaning could come from any of this. I did not care. I just wanted it to not be happening. I just wanted to hand Elisabeth's beautiful baby to her and tell her that in time she would forget about the pain of delivering her or him—the unknown, unnamed child.

Instead, I screamed into my empty hands so long the sun began to blister the edge of the world once again.

Life went on. At least it did for everyone except Elisabeth and her baby.

When I finally let my hands fall from my face, I saw the uncle holding Elisabeth's lifeless hands together atop the swell of her belly. I knew he was holding them in this graceful position to deny rigor mortis—or what locals call "the dance of death"—the chance to contort her too-small body into disturbing poses.

Rising, I tore a blood-stained sheet into strips. To avoid looking at Elisabeth, I kept my eyes busy—locked on the uncle. I grasped Elisabeth's hands and fumbled a strip round and round her tiny wrists. I tied a knot to hold them firmly in place. Keeping my eyes squared with the uncle's, I moved to Elisabeth's feet and held them while he repeated the ritual at her ankles.

We wrapped Elisabeth tightly in what remained of the blood-soaked sheet and loaded her given-out body into the bed

of our truck. The rough ride along the rutted road would lead us
away from the sun, toward her family's village where Elisabeth
and her permanently lodged baby would be buried.

Elisabeth's mother climbed into the bed of the truck and
lay prostrate over Elisabeth and the baby lodged inside her too-
small body. I avoided looking in my rearview mirror. Still, I
could hear the mother's hopeless wailing as she banged her head
on the side of the truck, and I drove away from the rising sun.

Cupping my face in his hands, Milton gently pulled my chin up, squaring our faces. My eyes floated to the pool of his and I cried, "Baby, I never knew a person could feel so desperate. I felt like I was dangling at the end of a rope from a thousand-foot precipice and there was no one to catch me. Not you. Not God. No one. I wished I'd died with Elisabeth and her baby.

"I wanted to call my mama. I wanted to cry myself to sleep in your strong arms and hear you tell me everything was going to be okay. I wanted to get drunk and forget I ever knew anything of Elisabeth, her baby, or that seemingly god-forsaken country. I wanted to run.

"So many times in my life, I had done just that. Run from truth. Hid from consequences. Anesthetized my pain. Blamed someone else. But this time, I had nowhere to run.

"It all happened so fast. One moment, I'd hoped to be this little girl's savior. In the flicker of a moment, like passing through a time warp, I felt like her murderer. Her blood will forever stain the way I see my hands.

"As badly as I wanted to run, shame kept me from even powering up my satellite phone to call you. How could I tell you I feared I'd just killed a twelve-year-old-girl and her unborn child?

"Something large of my heart died with Elisabeth. My voice went as silent as her cries fell. I couldn't even cry out to God. I think I was more afraid of your and God's comfort than I was your rebuking. How could I possibly receive comfort after what I felt I had done, or failed to do?

"I also feared that if you were too sick to travel to war zones with me, then what would the squall of my despair do to your health? I wanted to protect you from the horrors that kept me awake at night. So, I made the stupid decision to withhold my darkest and most painful days and nights from you. Like Adam and Eve with God, I hid from you.

"Since you've always been my only go-to man, I felt unfaithful to even consider sharing this darkness with anyone else if I hadn't first shared it with you. That left me to carry this—and many other dark secrets—alone."

That got Milton's attention, and for the first time since my tears and story erupted, he cut in: "Other dark secrets? What else is in there, Kimberly? What else do you need to tell me? I'm not going anywhere, and neither are you. You may be afraid you'll run, but I'll hold you. You're no quitter; you never have been. You won't be now."

Feeling spent, as if one more word from my mouth would snuff out my last breath of life, I laid my head on Milton's chest, drawing deep, jagged gasps. For the moment I could go no deeper. He put his arms tightly around me but pushed no further for words.

When my breathing steadied, Milton carried me to bed and undressed me while I marveled at the incomprehensible tenderness on his face. As he crawled under the covers with me, we both wept. We wept for the loss of Elisabeth and her baby. We wept for the long time I'd kept myself bound in shame and hidden from him. We wept for our sweet reunion.

In the midst of our tears, Milton made gentle love to me, mending my heart in all of its brokenness and tending the most barren places of my soul. I felt like Bathsheba when David came to comfort her after the death of their firstborn child—conceived in sin—and yet David comforted his wife through the grief. Through David's extension of himself, God blessed them with new life. I prayed for renewed life to course through me and give me the heart to offer Milton the whole of me in return for his unending love, compassion, and tenderness.

Long after Milton dozed off, I thought about how silence kills. I understood that when it came to the women and children I ministered to. I labored long and hard to build safe and loving relationships with them so that they felt free to unload their pain, loss, and fear with me.

"Share one another's burden" was my mantra with them. "Carry your own load" was as far as I could get for myself.

Somehow I rationalized that since my life was so much easier than theirs, surely I could shoulder these things alone. Now that I'd bled out the story of Elisabeth, I wasn't sure if I could contain the others threatening to erupt. My dark secrets refused to be contained—or die voiceless—as Elisabeth's baby had.

As the days passed, Milton would from time to time ask if I was ready to talk more. I was not. I struggled. Troubled weeks passed. I fought shame. I desperately sought a way to find freedom and still control consequences of the past. I wracked my brain over what possible good could come from unleashing so many long-ago swallowed, dark secrets. Yet, they festered more than I'd ever imagined.

Over time the stories of loss and suffering—both mine and others'—swelled so large within me, the knees of my soul bent placing my feet firmly to the floor, gaining leverage to push. The stories demanded their birth. I could no longer keep them bound.

Sharing Elisabeth's story opened a door I couldn't close, but it was like sticking my toe in a frigid ocean to determine if I would jump in or not. The stakes were high, too high not to take the leap. Still, I felt desperate as I searched for the courage to brave the icy waves ahead.

Chapter 18

WHEN THERE'S NO RAM IN THE BUSH

While my soul's feet were pushed to the floor, gaining leverage to birth what bound her, my body continued to go back and forth between Milton and Sudan. Sometimes I went alone. Other times, I led short-term mission teams. One time, when a short-term team had been on the ground only a few days, tension mounted as we faced a serious problem.

It had been a long, hot, dust-in-your-face sort of day. The team was frazzled by the heat, disoriented by culture shock, and out of sorts in general from having their daily diet calorically reduced by half and consisting of something like protein bars, peanuts, and water.

We'd come to Nyamlel to lead discipleship classes for the school teachers at our orphanage. We had scrimpy supplies. At the time, it was impossible to find even plain white paper in the market.

The desert floor became our chalkboards, sticks and fingers our chalk, and feet our erasers. Learning to make do with what was at hand created an empathic connection and deepened the bond between us and our Sudanese counterparts.

Grass roofs and thorny trees shaded us, but neither shielded us from the gale-force windblown sand that stung us like angry gnats biting through our clothes. Grit bore through the fabric of our pants and shirts; our socked and tightly laced–booted feet were the only parts of us that didn't chafe and grind as we moved.

When the day's work was done, and the wind stilled as the sun began to sink, I went to play a few rounds of volleyball with the children. With great drama I kicked off my boots, stripped off my socks, threw them inside out in the sand, and rolled up my pant legs just to see the reaction of the girls.

They all giggled, and the little ones rushed at me, touching the frog-belly white of my legs and lingering a bit over the blue trails of veins they couldn't see under their own thick dark skin. Beautiful, big-eyed Mary plucked up the courage to tell me she heard I was an albino, and asked if I would be okay. I assured her many people in America suffered the same thin-white-skin dilemma as I did, and most survived it for many years.

I've never been much of a jock, so playing volleyball in 125-degree heat with fiercely competitive teenage girls who towered over me quickly brought me to the brink of my physical limitation. I played three games and then begged to take the whistle where I could feign referee skills much better than athletic ones. I plopped my rear in the sand and cheered the older girls on, while the little ones mapped out the blue highways running through my legs.

As long as I watched and celebrated their great spikes and cried over their barely out-of-bounds losses, the girls really didn't mind losing my scant athletic ability. It was my attention they craved.

As for me, I always love every minute of being seen and celebrated that I can lavish upon the girls.

I stayed until the sun sank as low as the tops of the thorny trees before I left the girls. Heading to our campsite to meet the mission team for evening devotions, I promised the girls I'd return at bedtime to dance the evening prayers with them.

The youngest ones flocked about me, escorting me to the gate.

Hanging on my arms, they begged me to promise one more time that I would return to dance the evening prayers. I took a tiny, black, already-calloused hand of two of the girls, raised them high into the air, and twirled the girls around, assuring them I could barely wait for our nightly dance of worship.

"Me! Me! Me! Mama Kimberly, now me! Twirl me!"

So another ten minutes of twirling and swooning. Such a tiny gesture shared easily over just a few moments of time lit up these shiny faces with such joy and gave them hope.

As I passed through the gate back to base camp, a swell of sorrow filled my throat and pooled in my eyes to know that in such a hard land as Sudan, few could afford to stop the demanding work of staying alive long enough to share those simple moments and small gestures. Constantly fighting for survival left little time for the beautiful moments of life, like twirling a small girl and watching her face shine. I felt like the fair queen of many beautiful princesses to have the opportunity.

To Save the Ninety and Nine, or the One?

Walking toward the latrine, I heard two women's voices rise above the sound of the dry season's dead grass crunching under my feet. One was crying. One was speaking in soft cooing tones. When I stepped under the awning, I saw the crying voice belonged to our only female teacher, Atong, and the other to our girls' dorm lead caregiver, Mama Agnes.

Mama Agnes ran to me and grabbed hold of my arm. "Oh! Mama Kimberly! Praise Jesus you are here! You must help Atong."

Atong wouldn't look at me; she lowered her head and cried harder.

"What is it, Atong? What has happened?"

With her head bowed low, Atong opened up her story to me. "Nothing has happened yet. It is what will happen. My mother is dead. I belong to my father. I am educated, and I am still a virgin at nearly twenty years old. I will bring my father a high price. He has promised me to a corrupt businessman who already has four other wives. The man does not love me; he just wants me because I am educated and different from the other women. I am also young, and he knows I can give him many children. I do not want to marry him. I want to go back to school for further education and marry a young man at university whom I love. He has vowed to wait for me."

Sensing the weight of her pain, I asked, "Atong, have you told Lual Atak about this?"

"No. I have been begging my father for mercy to not make me do this thing. But now it is the end; my father has told me tonight he is sending me to the businessman, and my father will receive many cattle."

Atong dropped to her knees where Mama Agnes and I held her while we discussed what we should do.

Mama Agnes suggested, "Atong can stay with me. I will share my staff room with her in the girls' dormitory. She will become not only a school teacher, but also a caregiver in the girls' dormitory. It will be perfect; I need the help, and the girls love Atong."

It sounded perfect to me. I asked Atong what she thought of Mama Agnes's plan.

"Yes. I would like to remain with Mama Agnes, but I cannot. My father will put a witch's curse on me if I disobey him. It is a really terrible curse; I cannot face it."

I lifted Atong's face. For the first time since I found her crying, she locked her eyes with mine. "Mama Agnes and I will stay with you, teach you how to protect yourself, and show you more of what Jesus says about witches and demons and curses. There is protection from the witches' curses."

"Oh, Mama Kimberly, you do not know the Dinka curses. They are the worst. The Dinka witches are very powerful!"

"Atong, every night for many months the witches came outside our gates and cursed Lual Atak, me, and this ministry. We prayed and stood the ground that God had given us. The Dinka witches tried to curse us, scare us, or do anything to make us run away and abandon the children. They wanted them for slaves, or for pure evil.

"We never ran; and the curses never hurt us. Believe me—God is bigger than even the Dinka witches' curse. Can we at least tell Lual Atak and ask for his help with your father?"

"Yes. Please talk to him. I cannot; you must do it for me because my father will put the curse on me if I complain to James."

"Mama Agnes, why don't you take Atong to the pavilion, give her some tea, and let her rest awhile?"

"Ah, Mama Kimberly, that is a good idea. We will both take some tea. I will look for some biscuits, too. Would you like some tea and biscuits, Atong?"

Fettered by fear, Atong's chin once again sagged low on her chest, but she managed to nod her head.

Whose Ministry Is This Anyway?

When I went to Lual Atak, he immediately told me he already knew all about Atong's situation. He said, "Everyone is talking in the market about what a fine price Atong will bring her father. The businessman is very wealthy because he is also a big man in the SPLA. He has a lot of money, but he is a very bad man. In fact, not very long ago he beat up our compound manager and hurt him quite seriously."

Even more convinced we had to help Atong, I told Lual Atak the solution Mama Agnes suggested and about Atong's fear of her father's threat of the witches' curse.

Lual Atak surprised me with his response: "Atong is not a child any longer; she is a fully grown woman. She should speak her mind to her father and tell him she does not want to marry the bad businessman."

"You know what it is like to be a woman in Sudan. Atong has no power. Her father will do whatever he wants. You know that very well. She could be beaten, stoned, or put into prison for such a thing. How can you say 'she should speak her mind to her father'?"

Lual Atak wouldn't look at me. "How do I know? Maybe she even flirted with the man. She should have told him no for herself!"

Hair pricked up at the nape of my neck like the hackles of a riled dog. I felt Lual Atak's fear, but I did not know of what he was afraid. Confused by his lack of compassion—a side of him I'd never experienced before—I pleaded with him, "What is going on? You know what it is like to struggle here, how hard it is to stand alone, to be afraid. You have fought to save so many children. Why will you not help Atong?"

Like a coiled king cobra he sprang forcefully toward me. "If I help Atong, her father will lose a lot of money. He will be very angry, and he could have us all thrown into prison for disrupting his business arrangements."

"Atong's life is not a 'business arrangement'! We always say that we are here in order to protect those who are most vulnerable to human trafficking, and right now under our very noses one of our own staff is being sold to a man whom you yourself say is a very bad man and is known for beating people. If we just sit by and offer no help for Atong, then we are hypocrites and nothing we say matters. If we do nothing just because it is dangerous, then we would be doing good only when it is easy, or safe, or the price not too high."

"Kimberly, you do not understand! If we help Atong, her father may launch an attack on us, and I don't mean with witches. The bad businessman might buy soldiers to hurt us, or—Kimberly, you must understand—even the children. What you are asking me to do could start a huge fight where hundreds of people could be killed. You know very well this kind of killing happens in Sudan all the time. If we help Atong, then it could kill my whole ministry."

Lual Atak had me until that last line. That was what it all came down to. It was like God had us in a press, squeezing out every ounce of *self* He could get us to see—even the good self that wanted to save children. He was purifying us one battle, one choice, one life at a time.

I tried to explain to Lual Atak that this was the exact same decoy Satan had used to keep me from helping him years earlier. Everyone told me, "Don't help that boy. You'll certainly be robbed. You'll probably be raped. You may end up dead. But the one thing that is certain is it will kill *your* ministry."

I reminded James how afraid I was to help him. I was horrified that I would be robbed, raped, and murdered. I feared it would ruin everything Milton and I had worked for. But as Milton and I prayed about the words even our friends used, "Helping that Lost Boy—trying to build an orphanage in the war zone—will kill *your* ministry," they haunted us until one day we understood why, and made our decision.

"If it is *our* ministry, then it needs to die. If it is God's, we're not responsible for its success. We're only responsible to be faithful to what He asks us to do. And we dare not follow that path, no matter the darkness it will lead us through." It was as simple as that and, in good times and bad, we've never regretted it.

Now the same question returned full circle. This time it was for Lual Atak to face, and for me to help. "James, if this work is *your* ministry, *my* ministry, or a *donor's* ministry—anyone but God's—then as good as it looks or feels, it will all burn up like tall, dry grass in a desert wildfire. Please let go of *your* ministry. Trust God with the ninety and nine, and take the risk for the one—Atong. Please pray with me about what to do here."

"No. No. Wait. Give me time to think. I need to think about this. Our culture is different. Kimberly, you have spent much time with me and my people, but you still are not Dinka, and you still do not understand."

"I understand I may be killed for taking this stand. I understand everything we've worked for, including the children's safety, is at risk. I understand we may lose in the end because the bad businessman may still be able to overthrow us and take Atong. But more than anything, I understand that we cannot choose our actions based upon what we think will amount to success. We must choose our actions based upon what we understand God requires of us.

"Jesus left behind the ninety and nine—knowing the wolves may have attacked, even eaten, many of them—just to go look for the one who was most vulnerable. James, this is exactly why we are here. We are here for the one no one else will stand for. This is a testing of our commitment to our call.

"Please, just pray with me, seek God's direction here instead of holding on to what your, or my, culture says. This is not a question of your culture or mine. It's a Kingdom question. You take the time you need, but use it wisely, for Atong doesn't have the same luxury."

Our mission team was to gather for evening devotions in less than one hour. My heart was so heavy I wasn't sure I could lead. I prayed for God to show up in a way that would clear all the smoke and make evident to everyone how to respond to the life and need before us.

I did not pray for the father or bad businessman to back down. I felt barred from praying that; I believed God had brought Lual Atak and me to this exact point. We were being tested, asked to go deeper in our faith, rely more on Him and less on ourselves.

I also believed going through the fire would grow us together and close some cultural gaps by looking at how the Kingdom functioned instead of what either of our cultures would require. I couldn't help but wonder for what bigger battle we were being prepared.

The team gathered in our nightly devotional circle. Lual Atak straggled in late; his face grimaced with worry and fear.

Two Make Way Partners board members were on the short-term team. I knew they needed to know what was going on and what was at stake. In fact, everyone on the team needed to know, for everyone could be affected.

I relayed Atong's story and her plea for help. Lual Atak and I both explained our concerns and the potential repercussions.

Claudia, a MWP board member, immediately raised her hand and said, "I think we have to stand for Atong. I made my peace before I came here that I may not return alive. Here is the test—to risk saving the life of another."

Fred, also a MWP board member, remained silent throughout the meeting. Another woman on the team got stuck on the polygamy of the bad businessman. Lual Atak grew agitated and began a fearful conversation about how we could all die, and his ministry would be ruined.

We were all tired and needed a break, but I knew the clock was ticking for Atong. I proposed to Lual Atak something that I'd been struggling with all evening and that only my years in the desert—being transformed by God's broken heart for the oppressed—could have brought to my usually self-centered mind.

A Dangerous Plan

Negotiating uncharted territory, I laid out my thoughts: "I've been married a long time to a very good man. I've had the joy of raising children, loving grandchildren, and all the good things that life offers. Atong knows none of that; it all awaits her. Lual Atak, I would like for you to ask the bad businessman to give Atong's father the cattle so he does not incite war or seek to punish Atong. Let Atong go back to university to earn her advanced degree and marry the man she loves. But, to appease the corrupt businessman, I want you to ask him to take me in the place of Atong."

Springing from his seat, Lual Atak shouted, "No! I could never do that! You are too important to this ministry—to helping me and to saving the children! I will never ask him to do that. It is not possible."

Not surprised by his response, but certain of my stance, I reminded Lual Atak, "This ministry is not dependent on me; God has supplied all of your needs. My only responsibility is to be faithful with what He gives me. He has given me an abundant life, and now my life is all I have to offer to save one who has had so little life, but with so much ahead of her. I want you to make the deal with the father and the bad businessman."

The tension in our circle grew as thick as the lentil soup we fed our orphans. Knowing we were spinning our wheels, I suggested everyone prepare for bed, leaving the rest to James and me. I noticed Fred and Claudia went off to talk alone; James and I did the same.

"Lual Atak, I know you love me. I know you want to protect me. I know you would lay your life down for me, and I love and appreciate you for it. All I am saying is that I love and want to protect Atong in the same way you do me. The bad businessman will not take you; he might settle for me. Ask him. Please."

We both felt so passionately. We argued and pushed each other to consider the cost of either choice late into the night until we were both exhausted beyond words and found ourselves crying in each other's arms.

"I do love you, Kimberly. I will not trade you for Atong, but I will go first thing in the morning to her father and stand for Atong. I promise you I will do everything I can to save her. You pray for me while I go."

I wanted to go with him, but I knew, in such a time, my presence would make me the issue and thwart Atong's chance for freedom. I did not ask to go. Instead I said, "I will start praying right now. I will not stop until you return to tell me everything that happened, hopefully with Atong by your side."

I sat up in my plastic chair all night praying for James's courage, endurance, wisdom, and favor with the father. I reflected on a deeper level the words of Lual Atak when he told me so many years ago that I was like Esther, born for such a time as this. Only now, it was hard for him to play Mordecai as it came time for the one he loved to walk into the danger an Esther must face.

I was thrilled to see him slip out of his small house just after sunup, heading toward Atong's father's house. We did not speak; I only nodded encouragement and affirmation to him.

Painful Lessons

Still early—before the rest of the team stirred—Claudia roused from her tent. We walked and talked. She told me she and Fred had both been afraid I had gone off the deep end, and were scared to death until they got away from the circle and could talk and pray through the confusion they felt. They both received peace to stand for the one, Atong, whatever the cost.

As we waited for Lual Atak's return, both Fred and Claudia shared with me that the experience deeply challenged them to look at the difference between what they believed with words and what they were willing to put into action. They were both thankful.

Just as Claudia and I finished talking, I heard our truck roar into the compound. I knew it was bad news when I saw that Lual Atak was alone.

While we had fought, cried, and struggled amongst ourselves with what to do for Atong, she had fallen alone into despair and lost all hope. Fearing her father, witches, prison, and stoning, she had succumbed to the pressure and had gone to the bad businessman during the night.

We had lost the battle for Atong.

Sick with the loss, I hoped at least we'd gained a glimpse of Kingdom culture that would carry us beyond our own and prepare us for whatever battles lay ahead.

As I thought about being willing to risk my very life for Atong, two questions came to me: Why won't I trust God in the same way with my dark secrets? I trusted Him with my life; could I trust Him with my heart?

I didn't have an answer, but I knew the questions wouldn't leave me alone until they finished their work on me.

Chapter 19

THE SHAPING OF A
BUSH DOCTOR

After losing Atong, I headed home to once again attempt to claw my way out of the dark hole in which I'd buried myself. How could I go about righting all I'd wronged with Milton when I chose to hide what had happened to me? Yes, I had told him the story of not being able to save Elisabeth or her baby, but I kept hidden so much more.

How could I break the ties of shame and fear? Seeing God perform such miracles for the orphans, how could I not trust even Him with my deepest pain? I struggled, lost sleep, lost weight, and prayed for my own miracle.

Each time I left Milton for Sudan, and then returned to him weeks or months later, my reentry into life in the United States grew more difficult. And our reunions more strained. We went through all the right motions, but my hiding put a bridgeless gulf between us. Milton sensed something was very wrong—something more than the Elisabeth story—and it scared him.

Nearly every time I looked at Milton, he conjured the memory of my dark secrets, my hiding of the ugly things I'd endured and was afraid to expose. I built higher walls to protect myself, which meant locking out my husband from the deepest places of my heart.

Life at home was stressful in almost every way imaginable. Milton had several consecutive negative health reports indicating his diabetes was growing more serious. Nothing the doctors did, exercise, nor his strict diet seemed to help.

Finding a Safe Home, a Sanctuary

We had been running Make Way Partners from our home, but it grew to the point that we had no room left for ourselves except a bedroom. The straw that broke the camel's back came early one morning as I sat on our screened-in back porch with a cup of coffee. The sun scarcely topped the horizon while my prayers turned into tears. As I cried out to God once again over Milton's health, my fear, my secrets, suffering orphans, and how to reconcile the whole mess of life, a man pushed open the screen door and stepped onto our back porch.

Peering teary-eyed over my black coffee while clad in a flimsy bathrobe, I asked, "May I help you?"

With a huge smile exposing a mouthful of dentures, he said, "Oh! I'm sorry! I thought this was Command Central for Make Way Partners."

In that moment, I realized two things: Our home had indeed become Command Central for Make Way Partners, and the General could no longer lounge around in it in her bathrobe.

For the first time in quite a while, Milton and I took a healthy step in the right direction to take care of ourselves and our marriage. We decided to completely convert our existing home into the base of operations for MWP. We'd get a separate home for ourselves—a small, quiet place outside of town, preferably on a lake where we could enjoy our love of kayaking together.

Things began looking up. Within the year, we had turned our home into the official mission house for Make Way Partners and moved to a quiet lake an hour south of Birmingham. The move brought about several changes. The best change was to once again have a space where we could talk to each other without an employee or volunteer walking into the room midsentence.

The move and all that came with it went a long way to restoring our intimacy. Kayaking together brought my body back to life, and I no longer felt so anesthetized. But we still had a long way to go.

Limping Along in the Jungle of Life

Time raced by as our healing limped along. At the peak of our personal struggles, it was time for me to return to Sudan. Part of me felt angry for the impending interruption in our personal life; part of me was thankful to return to the lonely desert—a respite from the jungle of our emotions for a time.

We scarcely had time to admit how hard and lonely it was to be apart for so long and begin to reopen ourselves, and then it was time to separate again. Milton had begun to talk honestly about his fear of diabetes sapping more of his life until there would be nothing left.

His honesty pricked me to be vulnerable with him about how insecure I felt as a female leader in a man's world, and my fear of losing him to diabetes. Our disappointment with the church's response, or lack thereof, to the evil we fought weighed heavily upon us also. Two of our children were going through particularly tough rites of passage in their young adult lives. Every portion of our existence was in at least some level of turmoil.

As I battened down the hatches of ministry and household business in hopes of preventing either part of life from sinking while I went MIA for several months in a sequestered land, tension mounted within me … and in my marriage. No number of miles between us would bring relief from the nettles we had yet to pick from the fabric of our relationship. Instead I knew as always when I traveled, I would turn every conversation over in my head a thousand times—replaying them over and over again—hoping this time they would make sense.

I would keep asking God, "Are You sure I'm the one who is supposed to be here? I'm not qualified. I've made so many mistakes; You know the dark secrets I'm hiding. If this is right, then why is everything such a mess?"

The only response I ever sensed was, "Not everything is a mess. Children are alive who would otherwise be dead, because of this work. Keep going."

I wanted more. I wanted to see into the future. I wanted to know Milton and I would not have to live this way forever, with a great void of space separating both our hearts and bodies. Where was the Dynamic Duo who'd won that name our friends used to call us?

Now we were just barely hanging on day to day, trying to do the right thing, be faithful, and find our way out of a dark and painful mess that saved the lives of others while slowly sucking the breath out of our own. I vacillated from mild frustration to relentless despair.

The night before I was to board another plane carrying me from Milton's arms to Detroit, then Amsterdam, onto Nairobi, and finally Sudan, I knew I simply wasn't ready to leave him. We'd just begun talking; there was still so much unspoken hovering over us.

I cried in the basement for an hour as I stuffed my duffel bag full of protein bars, one change of clothes, a headlamp, emergency medications, and a sleeping bag. When I came upstairs, Milton had an open bottle of wine and a hot bath ready for us to share.

We sank low into the tub until the water sloshed slightly beneath our noses, just short of drowning us and just about to the same level as where our emotions had risen.

We talked until the water grew stone cold, and then we ran fresh hot water and talked some more. We told each other war stories. Mine from Sudan. Milton's from the home front. We laughed. We cried. And we remembered.

Milton dug Elisabeth's story from the tomb in my mind where I kept trying to bury her. He asked, "As you look back, can you see any treasure in the trial of living through losing Elisabeth?"

Dr. Conny's face filled my mind, the beautiful face of a woman I barely knew, but to whom, through our joint suffering, I was inexplicably bound. I met Dr. Conny when she answered a distress call to help me in the meningitis outbreak.

I raised my lips just above the water so Milton could see me smiling at him. How could I not love and trust this man with my whole being? Once again, he was drawing me into storytelling, knowing it was only through reliving the stories that shaped my life that I could discover the pearls of beauty God had sculpted through my dwelling in the dark shells of pain and pressure.

And so it was I remembered, relived, shared with my husband, and found a pearl of God's beauty formed in the darkness of a shared experience.

Two years ago, we'd done what had become our routine. Milton drove me to the departures curb of the Birmingham International Airport, and I'd left him alone, standing at the curb as he watched me disappear through the revolving doors. I remember praying for God's protection for both our hearts as we each did the best we could to be faithful in a hard call.

I'd clung to him through a sad substitute for conversation. Texting. My seven hours of travel within the United States yielded twenty-two messages fired back and forth, each full of hope, fear, love, pain, and loss.

Those twenty-two typed cries were followed by eight and one-half hours of silence while en route to Amsterdam. My five-hour layover in Amsterdam reignited the thumbing flurry of texting and yielded a dozen more messages. Neither of us said it, but we both knew the closer I got to Sudan, the thinner our line of communication would be. Another nine hours of silence as I flew from Amsterdam to Nairobi.

By the time I collected my duffel bags from the dirty conveyer belt, caught a taxi, and crashed in my tiny hostel, it was 1:00 a.m. My nights in Nairobi are always the worst. I'm exhausted but can rarely sleep. Alone in my one-dangling-bulb room, I fought the onslaught of demons accusing me of every failure, wrong choice, or selfish act I had ever committed. But even worse was my own second-guessing. "What am I doing here? Who am I fooling? Maybe I should just quit."

When 4:00 a.m. finally arrived, I put my struggles aside, showered, and stepped out into the gritty Nairobi air for a taxi. The pollution hung so thick in the air my nose immediately closed. When I opened my mouth to breathe, I couldn't smell the pollution, but particles from it landed on my tongue. I tried to clean it off by scraping my tongue against the roof of my mouth, but this only caused me to swallow the grimy, petroleum-based flavor.

Fumbling through my backpack to find my headlamp, I felt an envelope Milton had slipped inside before I left home. I knew it contained a letter filled with love and encouragement. I did not want to open it in the taxi. I'd save it for a time when I felt most alone in Sudan and needed to "hear" his love for me.

Strapping the headlamp around my crown, I flipped on the attached light. The taxi ride gave me time to thumb a few more texts with Milton. We both knew it was our last chance to say whatever we needed or wanted to say until I returned to Nairobi. Once in Sudan, my satellite phone would be too expensive to use, except for emergencies or quick check-ins to let him know I'm still alive.

As we pulled through the security gates of Wilson Airport, I powered down my cell phone, knowing it was good for nothing from here on. I culled through my backpack feeling the ridges of coins in the dark to sort Kenyan shillings from U.S. dollars for my driver.

Since my AIM (Africa Inland Mission) pilot was flying solo, he allowed me the prime view from his copilot seat. The small, rickety charter lifted off just as the sun leveled with the end of the runway. If a heavy heart counted as cargo, we'd never have been able to take off.

Two refueling stops and seven hours later, we set down in the desert on the border of Darfur—smack dab in the middle of a meningitis outbreak.

As I jumped out of the copilot seat, our nurse met me to report nineteen had already died within the last few days.

Suddenly the dense jungle of my relationship with Milton didn't look so dark.

More infected were flooding our small clinic every day. We weren't set up for this kind of crisis. Originally we had built the clinic only to tend the bumps and bruises of our orphans. Yet, being the only semblance of a clinic, the sick and the dying walked for days or were carried on homemade stretchers to reach us.

Despite the minister of health assuring us that additional help was on the way, days passed, and no help came. Another sat-phone call to the minister. More help promised. More help undelivered.

Giving up on the sat phoning for the time, I walked to our clinic. Key members of our clinic staff helped set up two other makeshift clinics in bombed-out buildings or under trees. Still, with no vaccine or IV fluids and limited antibiotics, it all felt pretty futile.

To make matters worse, government nurses gathered an assembly hot-tempered enough to rival the weather. Their chief complaints revolved around medicine and money. "President Bush sends money every month to our minister of health. She's supposed to build clinics, buy medicine, and pay our salaries. But our people die every day because we still have no proper clinics and no medicine. And we have not even been paid for our service in six months' time. Now she expects us to die of the meningitis while she gets fat on the money that is supposed to help our people!"

I empathized with the nurses; still, I wanted them to stay and fight for the children who were too weak to fight for themselves, and for the parents who needed to stay alive to provide care for their children. But the nurses had children and families of their own to consider. Most of them fled. Sad as I was, I could hardly blame them.

I had zero medical training but, trying to compensate for the lack of nurses, I immersed myself deep into a battle I knew nothing of. In three short weeks, our death toll rapidly approached four hundred.

Elisabeth and her baby represented just two in the echelon of thousands who wove in and out of our three makeshift medical clinics. Most of the people, like Elisabeth and her baby, died and left our clinic with their hands and feet bound in shredded strips of bedsheets we used to keep the haunting rigor mortis spasms from contorting their lifeless bodies.

On our darkest nights, too many died too quickly for us to stop our desperate fight for the life of another and bind up their lifeless hands and feet. In those times, we kept our gazes straight ahead—locked on our living patients—knowing the dead ones danced at the edge of our vision.

Once, while I worked to save an unbound dead man's wife, my eyes drifted and fell upon his arm just as it flung out in a gesture that gave me the eerie feeling he was calling his wife to join him in the frightful dance. I fought hard against his beckoning arm; in the end, it won.

Being so understaffed, our only method to sort patients was basic triage. The living who were not yet fighting the convulsions of death were pushed outside of our too-small, bomb-shattered,

crumbling clinic walls where they spilled out across the sur-
rounding ground. If they were rich enough to have a grass mat
to rest their emaciated bodies upon, they would lay convulsing
with fever, placing all their hope in the prayerful incantations
their families offered for medicine to arrive in time.

A lucky few actually rose from their mats and walked away.
They were saved by the scant supplies Dr. Bransford scrambled
together and flew in to us on short notice, using his own funds.

The thought of taking a daylong sabbatical to nurse my
weary soul seemed like an inhumane taxation upon the dying
who, if no medicine was forthcoming, would accept a loving
touch, a berceuse song, and a watchful witness to their suffering.
In truth, we'd become more hospice than clinic.

From his station in Alabama, Milton sought relief for
us night and day. Drawing from the Baptist World Alliance,
current supporters, and Dr. Patch Adams, he recruited an inter-
national emergency medical response team. I knew how hard
Milton had worked to get the team together; still, I felt in great
conflict about them coming.

They would arrive from Israel, America, Holland, and
Hungary. While we were desperately shorthanded, unless they
brought vaccines and antibiotics, the reality was their succor
would be minimal and their frustration high.

But by this time, I'd already lost Elisabeth and her baby.
Dropping twenty pounds in three weeks, I'd dimmed to a mere
shadow of myself. More important, my heart was dying. In an
effort to block out the pain, I had cut off my heart and could
not feel anything at all. I was more than numb; I was like a

prisoner on death row walking toward the electric chair—surely a dead woman walking.

Often, when late at night after crawling into my tent, I would curl up on my left side and let my right hand rest between my breasts as I fell asleep. Feeling the pulse of my heart, I would remember, I'm still alive. So, there must still be some mad hope. *I clung to those thoughts even when I could not feel them.*

Perhaps the thing I dreaded most about the team's arrival was my doubt about my stamina to lead, protect, and care for them. On top of my emotional fraying, my body revealed serious signs of wearing down. I sweated out several nights of unexplained fever, aches, and rash.

Even though I thought of Elisabeth and her baby daily, so far I'd been able to keep in motion. I threw myself into the work at hand with such fervor my exhaustion was practically intoxicating. While my hands whittled away at work, my mind lost itself in memories of Elisabeth, and I relived every strike I made in the lost battle to save her life. I refashioned them for each new patient I saw, hoping this time I'd get it right.

On the outside, I seemed fully functional. In fact, I appeared stronger than ever and led the pack in work hours logged. It was easy to work with the few indigenous nurses who remained behind, for they accepted life and death as it came. But to organize, orchestrate, teach, and direct a strong-willed motley crew of international doctors who had never even been to Africa—much less tied down the hands and feet of freshly dead, beautiful little girls whom they had fought to save moments earlier—was an altogether different issue.

Some team members couldn't even speak any one of our four commonly used languages: Dinka, Arabic, Kiswahili, or English. Translation issues would exponentially multiply frustrations for the team, our local staff, and our patients. As our death toll soared out of control, I knew the storm of anguish would rail against the team, and I feared it would create a squall of emotion taking me down with them.

In the end, with the stakes for the Sudanese so high, I decided to receive the medical team. I knew James wouldn't be much help, since he'd thrown out his back making midnight-ambulance runs with me through the rut-riddled paths to outlying villages.

When the team landed, though, James roused himself from his back injury long enough to join me in meeting them at the airstrip. We loaded all their gear into our open-back truck and hiked the couple of miles to the New Life Ministry compound.

Quickly dividing the team into two- to four-member response units, we assigned each one to their appropriate stations.

With James once again down for back rest, I climbed behind the pickup's wheel, squeezing Darlene and Jodie—team members with a history of bad backs—in the front with me. Exhausted from three days of travel just to reach us, a dozen other team members stood hanging to the thin metal rails framing the open-air truck while we tussled down the dusty, gully-furrowed roads to our first outpost clinic.

By the time we made it to the river, the sun waved half-mast in heat-rippled air. I stopped and climbed out of the truck to assess the lowest point for crossing. Our guard jumped from the back to manually flip our drive from two- to four-wheel.

Up until then the only time I'd driven across this river was alone, or with locals who knew the score. I stood upon the crest of its steep muddy bank, studying for the best spot to descend, the lowest water level to venture, and ultimately the path to climb its slippery opposite. Stories of trucks being swept away in such rivers—or stuck where bandits lay in wait—played in my head, nearly driving me to turn back for Nyamlel.

Charting my course, I slipped behind the wheel once again. My sweaty palms latched on as if clenching it would ensure proper navigation. Past failures dug up self-doubt as I considered this was my first time to cross with such cargo; the sense of responsibility for people who trusted me kept me focused on what I needed to do. They didn't want to die, and yet, they'd come a long way to do a job and did not want to turn back now.

I chose well going down the muddy bank and crossing the bumper-deep water. Climbing the slippery opposite bank proved a bit dicier. The truck's rear spun sideways, nearly jostling my tired passengers overboard.

The face of my brother, Ike, who took me mudding in his Jeep as a teenager, flashed into my head, and instinctively I did what I remembered him doing; I geared down, turned my front wheels into the nose of the spin, and pressed on. By the time we crested the tall bank, adrenaline roused me to joy, tears, and deep love for my brother who had taught me so much.

After another thirty minutes of eating dust as we bumped

*along the trails, we made it to our first outpost, Marial Bai.
I introduced the team to Eunice, the nurse in charge whom
MedAir had sent us from Kenya. I then assigned Dr. Jacoba
"Conny" Vrieling, a doctor from Holland, and Catherine
Broomfield Nelson, a nurse from Nashville, to work under
Eunice's watchful eye.*

*We operated our clinic in Marial Bai from a cluster of
bombed-out school buildings, which were long ago abandoned
due to lack of funding and teachers. I took careful note of the
team's wide eyes as we walked the grounds between the buildings and passed patients lying on hand-woven grass mats spread
under thorn trees.*

*Conny and Catherine were my main concern since they
were the two I would leave behind with nothing but a prayer
and a sat phone. Prayers could be used at anytime, but the
sat phone was to be saved for emergencies only. I knew that
for Conny and Catherine the oncoming night would soon feel
like a freight train running them down. As they hung IV poles
from tree branches, tied down the hands and feet of the ones
they couldn't save, and moved on toward the next lost cause,
they'd feel its steam burning at the napes of their necks.*

*Feeling antsy to make my return river crossing before that
freight train of darkness bore down upon us, too, I called for those
headed back to Nyamlel to load up. Nyamlel cradled her own
sick, about four hours away by "footing" or forty-five minutes by
truck.*

*With their introduction to healthcare Sudanese style, the
mood of our group fell solemn, but the return leg was blissfully*

uneventful. Just a few hours earlier, Nyamlel seemed like the end of the world to our team. Now, feeling the heat of the rougher edges burning around us, everyone seemed happy to be back in Nyamlel—where at least we had water filters and a grass fence for a sliver of privacy.

Nyamlel is a large village on the river near the border of Darfur, so it is the first host to many refugees, returnees, and a constant flux of soldiers. Our clinic focuses primarily on our orphans and is just too small to accommodate mass numbers of patients. As a result, our nurse established an additional make-shift clinic near the village market.

Immediately after the team set up camp, we went to work situating the two Nyamlel medical crews. No sooner had I returned from the village clinic when my sat phone rang. It was Conny. Even before I heard the distress in her voice, I knew this emergency phone call would not deliver good news.

As Conny relayed her situation to me, I thought of Elisabeth, and my heart broke for Conny, knowing what she was up against.

Like a pack of wolves circling their wounded in the wild, an entire family had walked through two days of bush to reach the closest clinic. In the center of their footed caravan they each held the corner of a blanket that cradled Auk, a young pregnant woman enduring heavy labor, and bleeding.

Conny told me she and Eunice examined the young woman and found placenta previa—a condition where the placenta delivers before the baby. Conny thought Auk's only hope for survival was an emergency cesarean.

Conny and I both knew she could not perform a C-section in the bacterial kingdom of Marial Bai's open-air clinic. She wanted to know the protocol. Protocol? I felt an insanely incredible urge to laugh mockingly, cry deeply, and scream wildly all at the same time.

Locking down my impulse, I told her the nearest place with a sterile unit was Aweil Town, two and a half hours away by truck, but it would take me another forty-five minutes to drive back to collect them. I also explained that while the distance was one issue, the greater concern for transporting a woman in Auk's condition was that the dirt roads between Nyamlel and Aweil Town were even worse than what she'd endured from Nyamlel to Marial Bai.

We'd have to be careful of the many land mines still riddling the area between us and our destination. And we'd have to drive through the river at night, increasing our risks of not only getting stuck but also of meeting up with bandits.

Conny was as undeterred to save Auk as I'd been for Elisabeth. I prayed her medical knowledge would accomplish what my ignorance had failed to.

I asked James to call a guard to ride with me. The guard and I set off for Conny and Auk. Just after crossing the river, we met the one ambulance for our county. The medic driving it agreed to follow us.

Skidding to a stop in front of the clinic, I was out of the truck before the motor stopped churning. Conny met me with determination; I could see the hunger in her eyes to save this young girl and her baby. I also felt her fear. I knew she already wondered—on the first day of her first trip to Africa—if she was in over her head.

I told her, "Everyone is in over their heads in Sudan."

As the family carried Auk out of the clinic to lay her into the back of the ambulance, my eyes played a trick on me. I didn't see Auk; I saw Elisabeth. She looked like a frail stick bearing a huge swell of sap smack dab in the middle of her length.

Our ambulance was a not-very-converted Land Cruiser. The only conversions were to rip out the backseats and drill in a couple of hooks on which to hang IV bags, if you were lucky enough to have them.

While the family squabbled about which two of them would squeeze in up front with our driver, Conny and I climbed into the back with Auk, fighting off the remaining family members who did not win the draw for up-front seating.

After two days of carrying their child, wife, sister, grand-daughter, and niece by the tattered corners of a blanket, they couldn't conceive of turning her over to two unknown kawaidjas. Knowing it was Auk's only shot—long as it was—we shoved her family back and slammed the ambulance doors as it sped off, literally leaving them wailing in its dust. Auk's husband and his older wife cautiously studied us from the front seat, their eyes sharing the tale of Auk, a family, and a people's suffering.

I sat on the hard metal floor holding Auk's head while Conny positioned herself at her feet. While Auk writhed in pain, Conny decisively went about hanging her IV bag, checking vital signs and blood loss. Before we even made it to the river, Auk rolled to her back, bent her knees, and used her feet to push

*her back off the floor of the ambulance—gaining leverage to
push hard. Conny tried holding her down and firmly warning
her not to push. Auk either could not understand or she simply
could not help herself.*

*No one in the vehicle spoke English except Conny and me.
My Dinka was far too limited to convince Auk of anything. I
tried to explain to her husband and his older wife. They seemed
to understand me, but Auk kept writhing and pushing.*

*Conny and I locked eyes when Auk began passing feces.
Conny caught it in her hands and passed it to my spare hand
to throw out the window. My other hand was busy holding the
pan into which Auk vomited. For several moments my hands
alternated throwing her bodily refuse out the window. Auk
streamed blood as well; Conny and I were both covered in her
bodily fluids. Even while I prayed for Auk and her unborn
baby's life, I confess that I also prayed for Conny and myself
to be protected from AIDS and other deadly transmittable
diseases.*

*Conny feared we wouldn't even make it to Nyamlel, much
less Aweil Town. Once we did arrive in Nyamlel, I asked our
driver to stop at the village clinic. Conny's fear bore true. Within
moments of carrying Auk into the clinic, she gave birth to her
stillborn son. Conny worked hard to revive the baby, but the
trauma had been too severe for too long.*

*This time, from the sidelines, I took in the entire scene,
including Conny. This focused, efficient, hard-driving doctor
who traveled many sacrificial miles to be in a strange and desert
land—leaving her own family behind—now stood stripped of*

her hope to save lives. Love, compassion, and grief flowed down her cheeks as she gently cried for the lifeless baby she held close to her breast.

Auk roused to insist that she leave the clinic to go home where she could bury her son. Heat sweltering even in the dark of night reminded us that he must be buried quickly. Both Conny and our nurse worked to convince Auk she must stay to recover from such trauma and loss of blood. Her husband intervened, insisting we return his wife to Marial Bai.

Within moments of losing her baby, we carried Auk to the soiled foam mattress still leaking her blood onto the ambulance floor. This time the son that had been bound in her uterus was now tightly wrapped in a shawl, lying in her arms.

As we retraced our dusty tracks to Marial Bai, the only noise heard above the thumping of the road was the hushed weeping from a mother too weak to wail.

Just as Conny feared, Auk's condition worsened during our return journey. As soon as the ambulance stopped, the back doors flew open with Eunice ready to take over. Full of experience and motherly authority, she took charge with the family, convincing them Auk's life was in jeopardy, and therefore, she must stay the night at the clinic.

Eunice, Conny, and the entire medical unit fought for Auk's life. At one point, her heart failed, and Conny saved her with a shot of adrenaline. She stabilized, and we all breathed a sigh of relief. It was late into the night, and our guard met me in Marial Bai to accompany me safely home to Nyamlel.

On my way down the bumpy road, I dozed and dreamed

*of young mothers dying before they could nurse their firstborn.
The faces kept switching between Elisabeth's and Auk's. I didn't
feel the truck stop, but I heard the crank of the emergency brake
as our guard yanked it up.*

*Sliding out from the passenger seat, I made a beeline for the
bathhouse, hoping to at least wash Auk's blood and excrement
from my face·and hands before collapsing on my cot.*

My sat phone rang before I made it back to my cot.

*Conny quietly cried on the other end. "She'd lost too much
blood. She was too weak. We lost Auk after all."*

*"I'm so sorry, Conny. You fought so hard. You did all you—
or anyone—could have done. Are you okay?"*

*"I'm not this kind of doctor. I am an oncologist. I'm not
trained or prepared for this sort of thing. What if this was my
fault?"*

*I knew that path all too well. "Oh, sweetheart, you tried so
hard! There was just nothing else you could do under these circumstances. This is not your fault. In no way are you to blame
for this senseless loss."*

*Conny conceded, "Right now, I'm just so tired and sad. I'm
uncertain of things."*

*As we hung up the phone, I promised I would return to
Marial Bai in the morning, hopefully after we'd both rested a bit.*

*Early the next morning, I once again found Conny hard at
work. I waited while she made her rounds so that we could talk
a bit. Finally able to sit with me on the broken cement steps over
which Auk had passed six times the night before, Conny shared
her burden.*

"I don't routinely perform emergency medicine. What if I gave her too much adrenaline—resuscitating her for the moment, but ultimately killing her? Perhaps she was too weak, and I should have done something else. Another doctor passed through this morning, and when I told him all I had done, he assured me I had done exactly the right thing, but still I ache so much."

I, too, assured Conny she'd fought the good fight. Beyond that, I knew there was really nothing more I could say. Knowing her deepest pain was not as a professional, but as a human, I just sat with her awhile.

Tears rose from her broken heart to her compassion-drenched eyes. We both knew the hard truth was that in either of our countries, Auk would have survived. Her gender, skin color, and nationality had practically sealed Auk's premature death.

With something as simple as adequate transportation to basic but clean medical care, Auk would be alive, joyfully nursing her newborn son as Conny and I watched with thanksgiving. Instead, Auk and her baby were both dead while Conny and I both railed against the injustice, but with an uncertainty as to what action to take.

After a few moments, we remembered the work ahead of us on this new day. Not knowing if it would include another Auk, or worse, Conny hugged me and walked inside the clinic. I stood in the doorway for a moment or two watching Conny and thinking leaders are never born but molded through the blood, sweat, and tears of sacrificial service. Conny was a beautiful, artful expression of leadership, and she was being further shaped by the Great Sculptor even as I watched.

Retelling, Reliving, and Reimagining

In the American Civil War, when surgeons sawed off the legs of wounded soldiers without anesthesia, commonly the pain was so severe the soldier's mind would shut down and he would black out. Oftentimes, emotional pain is just as real, and it causes the soldier's heart to black out or shut down.

As I finished retelling and reliving Conny's story with Milton, I realized I was that soldier. I was still up and running, firing my gun, but my heart had been in a blackout for nearly four years. Such severe pain had overcome me that my heart knew no other response than to shut down.

I began to reimagine my story. It occurred to me that perhaps I was no different than Conny. Perhaps I had done the best I could, and in spite of a terrible outcome, at least Elisabeth had died knowing someone had been there to fight for her.

I began wondering if perhaps we were all just doing the best we could. On some level, we're all "that soldier" with a shutdown heart. After all, humans weren't created to live in this hell; we were created for paradise with the King.

For the first time, the thought occurred to me that, while I stormed hell's rusted gates to free the oppressed, my dark secrets had been expanding hell's territory *within me*. It then made sense that if I wanted to bust down the gates of hell binding me, I'd have to come out of hiding. I began to imagine myself telling Milton ... everything.

In the tub, with half our bottle of wine gone, I confessed to Milton, "There's more I need to tell you. There's more fermenting within me. I just can't uncork it quite yet. I'm thinking this may be my last big trip away from you.

"I want to find a way to be both faithful to what God created me to be and faithful as your wife here in your arms. There's got to be a solution, I just don't know what it is yet. When I come home, I'll uncork everything, and we'll move on, I promise. Will you wait for me?"

Milton didn't have to say a word, and in his usual introverted fashion he didn't. Instead, he let his arms holding me tightly through the long dark night recant for the thousandth time his own story. Milton's story of unending patience, love, and devotion for Kimberly L. Smith.

Chapter 20

AND THE SAINTS GO MARCHING IN!

As hard as it was leaving Milton, I couldn't help feeling a certain hominess in Sudan. I had suffered with these people in ways no one except me and one other knew, and sharing in their suffering had somehow braided me into the fisted knot of Sudan.

God had certainly used this violent journey as a passport to make me part and parcel of this dark land, numbered among the suffering. Now, my mind would needle through the black nights of this trip, sorting out how I might be able to face Milton and tell him of the darkness that found—and bound—me here.

Many nights, while impatiently waiting for our orphanages to be completed, I'd lay flat on my back on a cot in the open air of the Sahara Desert. I tried to focus on the stars glittering like diamonds in the sky or the smell of smoke coming from our cooks' smoldering embers. But usually in the battle between my senses, my ears won.

Even the miraculous beauty of the stars couldn't compete with the heinous cackle of hyenas on the hunt when I knew so many of our school children were sleeping out in the bush.

I usually started the night lying on top of my sleeping bag with sweat dripping down my sides, soaking my bag. The outer nylon layer stuck to my skin when I rolled over, clinging like a web on a fly. It proved useless to pull it off; it would just stick to yet another part of my body.

Later in the night cool air marshaled a wind blowing low to the ground. The sand it carried would buffet my exposed skin like the mountains time has eroded through centuries of night wind, until finally I slipped down into my bag and pulled the top over my head. A fly caught in her snare.

Once asleep, I often dreamed of children scrambling up trees to claim their branches for the night—safe from the hyenas. The next morning reality would break in with the sun as I bandaged orphans from wild dog attacks or stitched their split foreheads from falling out of the high bough of their tree bed. Or worse yet, I counted the missing children of whom we would find no remains.

Living this life with the orphans made it easy for me to understand we must build safe housing for them, regardless of the risks or cost. It is not such an easy leap for those who don't hear the cackle, wipe off the blood, sew up the skin, or count the MIA orphans the morning after. Those who haven't seen or heard the orphans' life tend to rationalize the expense per unit, per child, per square foot against the fear of war potentially destroying their investment: a building.

Back Home Is a World Away

While in the United States telling the orphans' stories and seeking support to build a home for them, I focused on the investment being in children, not buildings.

When I met resistance to building in an insecure region, I asked, "If we knew our home would burn down next year, would we tell our children they may as well sleep in the woods now because we might have another fire next year?"

I openly shared my dream to save and protect as many children as possible, in spite of war and violence. Some laughed, some scoffed, and some simply turned away. Few encouraged us, fewer still supported the dream I was certain God laid on my heart.

At times, it felt impossible even *with* help; but with no real believers in the project, I began to question if perhaps I was just plain crazy, and everyone could see it but me.

Up to that point, even Milton wasn't committed. He hadn't been there. Hadn't held the children, wiped off their blood, or sewn up their skin. He believed in the theory, but Make Way Partners was very small: We had fourteen thousand dollars in the bank—which was needed for payroll and the food we'd already committed to buy.

The thought of building a multimillion-dollar orphanage, complete with security fencing, a clinic, and schools—two thousand miles away from our nearest supply chain—sounded foolish to those who hadn't seen or heard.

God used all of the doubt, fear, and questions to knit our board of directors tighter and more dependent upon His provision. We prayed earnestly as to what to do. All of us had the heart to move forward. Some of us lacked the faith and certainty to step out.

One Couple Leads the Way

One night after a long hard day of board meetings, I stayed up late speaking and praying with our vice chair and her husband, Louise and Steve Coggins. In the safety and comfort of their North Carolina home, Steve and Louise felt God tugging at their hearts.

They'd never been to Sudan, but God gave them a glimpse of what He feels every day as He watches His children suffer. The next day Steve and Louise took out a six-figure mortgage on their home, providing the funds we needed to break ground to build the first orphanage for Darfur refugee orphans and their counterparts in South Sudan.

From that moment forward, nearly three million dollars of orphanage homes, schools, freshwater wells, and clinics were built on the border of Darfur without ever a delay for lack of funding. So often we found ourselves scraping the bottom of the barrel, but God supplied just in time.

God moved in ways I'd never experienced before, and often not until we were at the end of our own rope! Once, I received a call from a man whose son heard me speak at a small church in North Carolina. Over the phone, he introduced himself as J. D. from Iowa.

J. D. asked, "What is your current greatest need?"

Of course, J. D. had no way of knowing that we'd just gone through an arduous process to determine if we should halt construction or order our next round of supplies from Nairobi. The needed supplies totaled $180,000, and we had less than $10,000 in the bank. Payment would be due when the supplies reached the border in a few days.

I told J. D. the whole story, our struggle with feeling irresponsible to order what we did not have the funds to pay for. Yet the more we prayed, the more we felt God urging us to press on and look to Him. So, shaking in our boots, we did just that.

J. D. told me he would talk with his wife, Pam, about how they might be able to help and hung up. The whole conversation lasted less than ten minutes.

Two days later J. D. called back to ask for our bank-transfer information; he and his wife were sending the entire $180,000 because they felt like we'd stepped out on faith. They believed God was calling them to be the answer to that faith step.

Pam and J. D. wanted no special attention; they wouldn't even allow me to tell the board who gave the money. Although it would be quite some time before we met face-to-face, J. D. and Pam responded similarly several times over the years.

Contagious Vision

Over time, as God kept supplying both funds and safety, and progress began springing up against unbelievable odds, other groups joined in. African Leadership was the first to join the cause. They invited me to speak at their annual banquet and gave their donors an opportunity to support the orphanage. African Leadership not only helped with the brick and mortar, but to this day they continue to help with the ongoing costs of maintaining that first orphanage through their Mocha Club.

Voice of the Martyrs has provided vehicles, medicine, foot-powered sewing machines, Bibles, blankets, and many other beautiful gifts to expand our orphan care.

Randy Alcorn and Eternal Perspectives Ministry (EPM) not only support our work with orphans but also open the hearts and checkbooks of literally thousands of believers through Randy's books, newsletters, and the EPM website.

Open Doors supplies funds for our school buildings, and the director for Sudan, George William—having led James Lual Atak to the Lord years earlier—remains a great friend and encourager to him.

We can always count on Dr. Dick Bransford of BethanyKids to

help with emergency medicine or surgery on babies and widows we smuggle out of the country.

Focus on the Family has been a huge help by sending a documentary team and airing broadcasts to give Christians positive ways to respond to such evil.

And then, there's Africa Inland Mission (AIM). Without AIM and the pilots who fly us in and out of remote areas landing on packed strips of desert floor, it would not be possible for us to do what we do. These bush pilots risk their lives day after day, year after year, in order to get missionaries where we need to go to answer the call God has placed on our lives. More than once they've flown in on a moment's notice to get one of us who had fallen hard to malaria, pneumonia, or some other ailment threatening our lives.

Many other churches, foundations, businesspeople, and believers at large climbed on board, rising from what seemed a barren wasteland. It was quite humbling to watch God mobilize a motley crew of His children to care for His most vulnerable orphans. Within eighteen months we moved nearly 250 girls into their new home, followed by nearly 250 boys within another eighteen months.

Not a Soul in the World for Little John

Just when I was beginning to feel confident we'd done a good thing and could coast awhile, a little boy standing on the side of the road in nothing but a tattered shirt captured the eye of my camera. We sped by him en route to an Internally Displaced People's (IDP) camp. He was alone and miles from any village; I wanted to stop, but it wasn't my call.

We were experiencing severe flooding and were taking the area commissioner to the IDP camp so he could meet thousands of people who'd lost their homes, crops, everything. He said he was on a tight schedule. We did not even stop to talk to the boy.

Some days later, en route to the same IDP camp, James and I stopped the truck to walk along the road looking for people who'd fled their homes to escape the floods. Again on the side of the road, I saw him. This time I knelt down to meet him. He wore the same threadbare shirt and nothing else. He told me his name was John, and he thought he was five years old. That is what his mother told him before she and his little sister died.

John's eyes appeared vacant, and his voice never altered its timbre as he told me about his little sister, Abuk. She died first, and then his mother stopped eating so she could give all of the food she found to John. John's mama died soon after Abuk.

For a split second I thought perhaps John was going to cry, but then he began talking again. John didn't cry when he told me how his mother died, lying in the bush with only little John at her side. Her chest rose and fell less and less until it didn't anymore. He just said that he missed her because she was his only friend since his father died before John was old enough to know what killed him.

I asked John if he wanted us to take him down the road to the IDP camps so that others might help him. His eyes grew wide, and I saw genuine terror in them. His little body ever-so-slightly recoiled from me.

He said that his mama told him that he would be safer in the bush than in the camps where the militia went to get new slaves; John did not want to become a slave. John's mama told him it was better to die a Christian in the bush than live a Muslim in slavery.

I pulled James aside to ask him if we could take one more orphan into our orphanage. He reminded me that just the day before I had told him that I was concerned that he'd taken in fifty new orphans since I had last visited him and that we still didn't have enough sponsors to take care of the ones we already had.

I had told James I knew it was very hard for him to watch the orphans around him starve to death or be vulnerable to slave raiders and hyenas, but we simply could not take more in until we had provision for our current nearly five hundred. Through tears, James agreed not to take more orphans.

Now, here I was facing what James faced every single day of his life.

I recalled the final scene in *Schindler's List*. Schindler weighed the cost of his watch, his car, and every single possession he'd clung to against how many lives he could have saved if he had let go of those "precious" possessions.

I considered the unbearable weight of grief that James must feel every single day. My mind measured what it meant to leave little John on the roadside, where he felt safer than in the IDP camps. My heart could not contain it.

Now being beyond tears, I knew I had no right to violate what I had just asked James to commit to so that my conscience was clear, or to save the one who tugged at my heart when James had to turn masses away every day. Again, the impossible predicament …

James and I prayed together over little John. I promised John I would tell others about him. He wanted to know "who" I would tell and what they would do. I told him that there were too many people for me to tell all of their names but some would be black like him, some would be white like me, some would be brown like the Arabs that he was afraid of, but that all would pray for him.

I gave him a blanket and all the food that was in my bag.

John smiled. We climbed into our truck leaving a smiling orphan with a bloated belly standing on the side of the road. James and I both cried all the way to the IDP camp.

Many More "Little Johns"

The first time I published Little John's story in the Make Way Partners' newsletter, we received more written responses to his story than anything we had ever shared. Most of the responses we received ran along the lines of, "If you'll go back and find John, I'll commit to sponsor him."

I realized my article had failed to communicate both the depth of despair that the masses of orphans are suffering in Sudan and the height of power that we have to change their reality. So I tried again.

The heart of the responses was right on. Jesus certainly teaches us to go save the "one lost sheep." However, in Jesus' story, he said that there were ninety and nine safe and one was lost. In Sudan today, it is more like we have one safe and the ninety and nine are all lost! As George Müller lamented in his memoirs, "In our world today, the numbers are nearly reversed."

I'm not calloused toward Little John. My heart still breaks for him. James and I often speak about him. To this day, we scour the roadside for him as we drive along. James is more heartbroken than any of us as he looks at hundreds of "Little Johns" every day outside our safe orphanage walls. They cry to get inside where there is a protective fence with loving teachers and good food.

James is the one carrying the weight of walking by them and saying, "No, little one. I am sorry, but I don't have enough money to feed all of the ones we have inside. We have no room for you yet. I will call for you when we have met our current commitments."

So many are begging to come into our safe orphanage. I cannot ask James to go get Little John, bypassing all of the little ones that he would "step over" to find Little John. John is not just some poster child. He is real, and he is suffering. Yet, he does represent masses of children in his exact same situation.

Because literally thousands of people began praying for Little John—and many still are—I can only hope that wherever he is, he feels some sense of God's comfort through those prayers. Little John, you are not forgotten.

New Territory

Even while we celebrated moving our orphans into their new home, Little John's face weighed on me day and night. It was time to move forward, making way for more housing to care for the countless orphans still barely hanging on in the bush. But we needed more than just one reliable indigenous leader. It would take many more like Lual Atak to accomplish all God had put on our hearts.

Fred Blackwell, a director for MWP, and I flew into Torit, Sudan, to meet with three pastors who had undergone African Leadership's leadership training. I'd known this band of brothers for several years, and they fit our leadership bill perfectly! Within days we secured two hundred acres, along with the dream to build homes for five hundred more orphans!

The three pastors explained they were *Charlie Mikes*. I asked them to repeat it several times as I couldn't quite make out what they were saying. Knowing they commonly mix English, Arabic, Kiswahili, and Otuho all in the same sentence, I asked, "What language are you speaking?"

Howling with laughter, "English! Of course. We are saying, 'Charlie Mikes.' Crazy Men—Crazy Men for Christ!" Like a light going off, it dawned on me that in the phonetic alphabet "Charlie Mike" was "CM."

I would soon learn Charlie Mikes was a name hard earned by these three, and they made me want to be more of a Charlie Whiskey, Crazy Woman for Christ!

Satisfied with the great work God was doing through James Lual Atak on the border of Darfur, and deathly ill with a wicked case of malaria topped off with pneumonia, I headed home to tell everyone about the Charlie Mikes near the border of Uganda and to receive medical care.

Slowly, I began to accept that I had done hardcore pioneering work for nearly five years in Sudan, the preparing of the way for others. Others who were either single or had their mates by their side. Milton and I—our marriage—had paid enough.

It was time for me to go home. Time to accept my call as storyteller, testifying to the oppression and injustice I'd witnessed and experienced; time to be reunited with my husband, closing the deep gap—carved in part by my dark secret—that still plunged between us. Praying for God's strength and mercy, I headed home.

Chapter 21

ANOTHER PIECE OF
GOD'S HEART

Once I returned to the United States, days, weeks, and months passed as I wrestled to find the courage to speak. I could only seem to dig so deep into my cave of dark secrets, nestle my fingers around the truth, and pull just enough to inch it a bit closer to the light. Then fear would grip me, and I'd be that soldier blacking out all over again.

I feared the cost of a clean conscience would be too high. On some level, I tried to control the outcome. On another level, I seemed to have no power to choose differently. I wanted to make sure that if I told Milton all of the secrets I'd been hiding that, first, it would not take his health down a worse road than it was already heading. But, second, I wanted to know that he'd still let me go back to Sudan, to the people I was numbered among. I felt the hard times of working in Sudan—and being away from Milton—for months at a time were past, but I still felt a strong need to stay in touch with the widows and orphans I'd grown to love and promised to visit.

I feared the thread Milton would pull from me would be the very one God had woven between the people of Sudan and me. If that thread were unraveled, I felt the threadbare afghan of my ragged soul would surely come completely undone, leaving me stone cold. So, I continued to hold back.

I rationalized if Milton was too sick to travel with me, he must also be too weak to deal with the dark and painful parts of what I faced while away from him. I knew he loved me; I knew he loved the

Lord. I'd watched him go through a life-altering process of submitting to God and eventually turning me over to Him, even to go to a land where rape was a sanctioned weapon of war.

But I also knew he was human, and distinctly man. No matter how good the reason, it hurt him for me to travel to a war zone without him. It cost him something. I knew it would hurt him even more, cost him even more, if he knew the extent of what I had endured without him.

Along quiet moments of every day—alone in my car, sitting in an airport, doing housework, or as I drifted off to sleep at night—I thought of Conny and Auk. I was clear neither Auk's nor her baby's death could be placed upon Conny. Yet, I hid the things I did because, somehow, I felt I should've been able to save them. I felt deep shame.

I read countless books searching for mentors to guide me in facing my ugly underbelly where I'd stuffed the shame. I read practically everything Elisabeth Elliot ever wrote. The books were inspiring, yet they felt, to me, so full of guts and glory that I just couldn't relate. I fell so miserably short of her example; I felt it too far a leap to even consider.

With my bold mannerism and endless travel, people often compare me to the "Tramp for the Lord," Corrie ten Boom, but from everything I read of her, she'd always chosen light over darkness, good over evil, honesty over lies. I needed to glean from the saints who also showed us their sin.

So I turned to more current true-to-life Christian stories. While they weren't the same powerhouse guts and glory, it seemed as soon as each of the women found Jesus, their problems went away and they became instantly sweet, loving, loyal wives, mothers, and churchgoers. Again, I just couldn't relate. I had Jesus. I'd given my life to serve Him in ministry. Still, I felt everything was crumbling down around me.

Where were the books about the real people who found Jesus but still kept sinning, failing, fighting, and struggling against themselves throughout their lives, as the good work was being completed? Every modern-day story I read seemed like the people went from zero to one hundred, getting their act together the minute they "got Jesus."

Struggling with what to do with the mess I'd made of life, I left the "true-to-life" Christian stories behind in search of my own.

God's Dream of Me

At the back end of some meetings in Colorado, I scheduled a few days alone in nature. The day before my wilderness time began, a friend asked me, "What did God dream of when He first imagined Kimberly L. Smith?"

As I scrambled for an answer, all I could see were the fists of guilt, shame, pain, loss, and anger that seized His dream of me. All the pain and guilt for failures in Sudan clanged in my head so loudly I could hear nothing of what God might think of me. I was so focused on how I saw myself, I was clueless as to how God saw me or all the lives He had saved and healed through me. That scared me more than the shame.

I rambled for a few minutes about some childhood memories of being happy and feeling free. My friend knew I was faking as I searched for something, anything. Finally I admitted, "I haven't a clue."

Early the next morning the wilderness time I'd set aside began. Still in my hotel room, I started long before the sun rose by writing in *Reflections on Your Life,* a guided journal by Ken Gire.

Gire's first directive is to *read the moments* of our lives as they happen. As I read the moment of my life relating to my friend's question, I began with how I saw myself. As I looked at the words scrawled across my journal's pages, I was shocked at the vile images filling my head about myself.

Guilt and shame had turned to self-hatred and blame. Together, they not only colored how I saw myself, but also how I perceived Milton—and even God—looked at me.

The thoughts were crushing. I sobbed as bitterly as when Elisabeth and her baby died; only this time I cried for the death sentence I lived under. And the one I imposed upon my precious husband.

As the sun rose, I packed my gear and headed out to hike high up a nearby mountain. I laid outstretched on a dam holding back a reservoir. The wind bit cold upon my face, but the sun eased its sting as I considered the tremendous force of water held back by the dam I rested upon.

It was a fitting metaphor for the retaining wall I'd built to shield Milton, my children, friends, James—everyone in my life—from really seeing me. From behind its height, I hid my sin, pain, shame, and fear.

I felt so ashamed I didn't know where to turn. Who would receive me? In the wide-screen theater of my heart, God began to show me the depths and darkness of my sin and how it affected others. I'd seen and confessed my sin before, but I had never seen the degree of darkness within me that God showed me on that day.

Surprisingly, the sin He revealed to me had nothing to do with Elisabeth or the other stories I'd hidden in the dark cloak of shame. My sin had much more to do with my selfishness, my trying to control, my unwillingness to risk what really mattered to me: relationships. Above all else was the shielding of my life from my beloved husband.

I felt the grip of shame clutched around my heart begin to come undone. Wonder trickled in as I considered maybe the things I feared telling Milton might not be completely my fault, or mine to carry alone.

While my body shook in brokenness, God began to show me something else. He showed me how He saw me.

Beautiful Dancing One. Gentle One. Art in Motion. Lover of My Heart. Seer. Accepting Lover. Tender, Gentle One. Lover of Life and People. Warming Fire. Confident. Faithful One. Resurrection.

Name after name swept through me, each one taking me deeper into His love and vision for me. I cried, realizing how God sees me is contrary to every bit of self-talk that fills my head, drives my actions, and forms my days.

God affirmed, in the blackness of my sin; He saw me in that very moment—not some far and away distant day *if* I could ever achieve it—as Beautiful Dancing One. Faithful One. Resurrection … and all the beauty He dreamed of as His great sculpting hands first formed me.

God called me faithful even as I strayed and attempted to cut Him out by controlling who knew what, and thus, who could do what.

Earlier in the morning, when I first set out on my hike, I'd planned to climb another thousand feet to a national forest land. As

I lay there, listening to God, feeling His love for me, knowing His vision of me, I spent every ounce of energy I had.

Still, I struggled with letting go of what I had planned for the day, afraid I was stopping short or missing out on something else, until I heard God say, "This is far enough for today. It's okay to rest. You will make that climb another day."

I lay in the woods crying, receiving God's heart for me, and writing every word of it down so as to never forget it. Psalm 139:14 came to me. "I praise you, for I am fearfully and wonderfully made. Wonderful are your works; my soul knows it very well."

I am one of those works!

And my soul knows it very well!

As I hiked down from the reservoir, I felt radiant ... like Moses climbing down from Mount Sinai. I put my hands to my face wondering if it glowed.

An Abiding Place

There are many remarkable days in my life. The day I first knew I was in love with Milton, and he with me. The mystery of feeling new life flutter inside me as my babies grew and stretched within.

The day I glimpsed how God sees me is certainly among them.

Coming down off the mountain also turned my mind toward going home and facing Milton. I had so much to confess. I knew he had not had such a mountaintop experience; he would be in a different place. Insecurity crept in, threatening to uproot all the things I learned on the mountain. I read my journal several times each day to reinforce and keep ever-present in my mind the profoundly intimate message God gave me.

I read the John 15 "abide in me" passage over and over again. I once heard a man substitute the words "cling to" instead of "abide in." I wanted to cling to God's image of me and resist the lies I'd fallen into.

Down off the mountaintop, though, the work was much harder. It was an all-out fight.

The meanest demon to face smoldered within me.

Clinging to His truth, I began to find the courage to speak mine.

Returning home, I knew I could not wait another moment. Suddenly, the very events I'd once classified as unspeakable moved under the contractions of my heart—pushing, demanding to be birthed, held, and given voice.

It was time to confess to Milton the whole ugly mess I'd made by hiding so much of the journey through which God had carried me.

Chapter 22

STOP SHIELDING,
START SHARING

Milton knew about Baby Elijah; he did not know what happened to me when I went out to find him. I decided that was a good mess to start with.

Just one day after placing Baby Elijah in the home of his new caregiver, the second of the two women who had originally brought him to us returned to our compound and requested to see me.

She told me that the woman we'd entrusted Baby Elijah to had been overcome with fear fueled by the local custom, had not fed him once in the last twenty-four hours, and had returned him to the bed in her tukel where he waited for death to carry him to his mother.

The woman before me wrung her hands both in worry for Baby Elijah and in fear of the repercussions for coming to me. She wanted to alert me, but she was too afraid to take me to the tukel where he lay.

I looked for James. I powered up my sat phone and tried to call him on his, but an hour passed and he was nowhere to be found. It would be dark in another couple of hours, and I knew it would take time to find Baby Elijah. None of us knew which tukel was fast becoming his tomb.

I set out walking alone to the market—hoping I would find James, or anyone else who could help.

The three-digit temperature summoned sweat from every pore of my body, soaking my shirt and plastering my hair to my scalp. Still my body trembled with fear. I wriggled my way through the crowded stench of the market. Dinka people towered over my five-foot-seven-inch frame.

Feelings of smallness, insignificance, and panic overwhelmed me as I pushed my voice above the height of the crowds, "James! James Lual Atak!" I knew if James just heard my voice he would come running.

I rambled through each dirt path swathed between the crumbling market tukels and rickety plywood stands. Stares of resentment for me—the kawaidja woman who had enough money stashed in her tent to solve the sum total of their problems for years to come—filled me with guilt. The appreciative smiles and warm touches from widows who knew and loved me well but could speak no English to help me brought comfort and faith to continue.

I wondered if James went to a quiet spot to watch the sunset as we sometimes did. I rounded the last fray of grass huts defining the borders of the Nyamlel market. Making my way down the rutted divide toward the river, instead of finding James, I caught the attention of a pack of men dressed in white Islamic gowns.

Fear flushed me. I turned to run back up the hill. My boot slipped in a patch of mud, landing me facedown. Before I could get my hands under me to push my way up, they were on top of me.

I tried to scream. All that seeped out between their kicks stabbing my back were weak mewls and grunts of pain and terror. I fought to get my arms under my body so that I could push myself up. I held to the illusion I could still run away. I fought harder.

Men on each side of me grabbed my arms, crushing them into the dirt. More pushed my face in the mud where my boot had failed to take hold. Still more grabbed my feet and splayed my legs, binding me while the pack kicked and punched me.

Someone pulled at the back of my collar but they could not strip off my shirt with so many men holding me down. With a swift jerk, they flipped me over on my back, my head hitting hard on the ground. Sharp blows then came at my face, breasts, sides, and thighs.

I knew I would be raped. By the whole pack—one by one—with each one watching, laughing, kicking, and celebrating my humiliation.

Men on both sides roughly pulled my arms up and over my head. I felt my shirt ripped from my body. Hands tore at my pants. Others mauled at me. Then, one by one they began ... each one angrily taking his turn at me. A scream finally rent from my throat.

I knew I would be mutilated.

I hoped they would kill me.

So many towered over me that their bodies formed a coffin around me, burying me from seeing the sky. All I could see were white robes and black faces of hate. I had little strength left to struggle against them.

Milton's face came to me. How it would break his heart to

see this, know this. I fought harder to get up, rail against, and squirm out from under. The massive effort gained me nothing.

Some kicked dirt in my face while others spat both words and spittle at me. I could not understand the words. The evil and hate they hurled at me had a language of its own that transcends all race and nationalities.

I tried to make my mind focus. I searched for solutions to questions I wouldn't be around to answer. Milton is such a quiet man of solitude; who would be there to comfort him through this?

At some point I must have blacked out for a moment, or longer. I roused to rapid machine-gun fire.

Suddenly a space of sky opened to me as men toppled over one another, and they lost their grip on me. Green camouflage pushed more of my attackers over and reached down to me. Camouflaged arms picked me up as a dark black face, belonging to an SPLA soldier, grimaced at me.

The SPLA soldier carried me up the hill, sat me down, and gently wrapped my shirt around me. The buttons were gone, but I slid my arms in the sleeves and pulled it tight to cover my breasts. I clutched it together with my left hand as I stared between my soldier's legs to see if the men followed us. None did. I gathered my pants together, nervously groping at them with my right hand because the zipper teeth were stripped.

He pointlessly rushed a slew of Dinka words at me. I tried English; it was hopeless. So I just cried, held my clothes on tight as I rocked myself, while repeating "Baby Elijah" over and over again.

My soldier friend reached down to help me stand, balanced me under his shoulders, and walked me out of my attackers' view on the outskirts of the market, back to New Life Ministry.

James was still not back from wherever he had gone. I put on my only other set of clothes and collapsed on my cot thinking I had failed. Baby Elijah would surely die in the night.

I lay awake on my cot in fear of what the night held; I prayed James would come back soon. Together we could find Baby Elijah.

As I prayed, I saw two figures moving toward me in the dark. I sat up.

As they drew near, I saw two women. One carried a small bundle in her arms. Against all hope, I stretched out my arms in hope. I received my reward—Baby Elijah—who began crying as soon as my arms pulled him to my bruised breast.

This time I did not have to revert to the eyedropper. His mouth groped for the bottle's nipple as soon as he smelled the milk coming toward him.

When James finally returned late in the night, Elijah and I were both hard asleep on my cot. In the black of night, James could not see my face. He woke me and tried to convince me to let one of the helpers care for Baby Elijah so I could rest. I had no intention of letting go of him again, not on this night.

In the morning, I cleaned myself up a bit. My bottom lip was torn open, and my eyes were colored and swollen; but most of the cuts and bruises were on my back, thighs, and torso.

I was afraid to tell James what happened for many reasons. Chiefly, I feared James would look for the men, kill them if he found them, and start an all-out war from which no SPLA soldier could save me or the orphans.

Then I began worrying about the pain and stress all of this would cause Milton and how that would affect his diabetes and organs.

I had also encountered so much prejudicial thinking against Africans that I was afraid if our supporters knew what happened, they would judge the Sudanese harshly and withdraw their support. I had been told many times I was a fool for trying to build an orphanage in Africa. Often people said, "Those Africans have always been killing each other, and they always will kill each other."

It was so complicated and hard to explain. "God is here, He is working, good things are happening, but sometimes I do stupid things like go out by myself, or run-amok evil just takes over—no matter where you are."

Besides, it wasn't Africans killing each other. Arabs invaded Africa and were killing the Africans and taking the spoils.

My clothes covered all my cuts and emerging bruises, save my purpling right eye and the jagged tear running from the left corner of my lower lip down to the bottom of my chin.

When James roused at his usual 9:00 a.m., he gasped at me, "Mama! What has happened to you?"

I lied, telling James I fell down the hill at the river and hurt myself. I was thankful he didn't ask more questions.

By the end of my story, which was really our story, Milton sat stone silent. I was afraid to move or even to look at him.

Finally, he broke. "I knew you were hiding something! How could you keep this from me? You're always controlling what you let me see, how much you let me know. From the very beginning I knew you were not ready to go to Sudan. You didn't even really ask me. You came to me, but you never really asked. In reality, you dared me to tell you no! You were on the fast track to go, and you know it. You would've gone with or without my blessing, and now look what has happened!"

I knew he was right. I'd always only given voice to my fear. I hadn't talked about the fact that I wanted to go to Sudan and right every wrong—in my own strength. Still, knowing he was right, I couldn't take his yelling at me at that time. I broke.

Grief burst out my throat as if death itself was clawing its way out. I felt disconnected from the noise I heard. I couldn't fathom that such agony came from me. Even in Sudan, I had not quite heard such a dreadful sound.

Suddenly, I realized Milton had gathered me into his lap, and we were both sobbing in each other's arms. He was hurt and angry that I had carried this alone for so long. He also knew I had been traumatized and met me with the merciful understanding that people often don't make the best choices in those times.

Milton's tears singed my heart as he mourned, "I'm so angry with those evil, evil men. They had no right! I keep thinking of the story Nathan told to David when he confronted David for taking Uriah's one little lamb—Bathsheba. Those savages had no right to hurt my one little precious lamb. You're my precious little lamb. I wish I could have died instead of them hurting one hair of your beautiful head."

That was the first of many nights of remembering, grieving, crying, and making way for the long and rocky road to healing we would walk together.

A Deeper Understanding

The first twenty years of marriage I'd restricted the concept of being "one flesh" to the sexual. As I felt the way Milton shared my pain and reflected on the way I'd been holding so much pain for him, I began to consider being one flesh on many different levels.

I'd long understood that when I went to Sudan and Milton remained at home, he carried a great weight and suffered in all ways, and in all times, with me. I knew he fasted at times and interceded often, literally asking God to take him out in order to spare me if I were in harm's way.

I'd never seriously considered how his disease and loss of so much life force had likewise affected me. I'd always looked at Milton's diabetes as *his* disease. I thought I must find ways to nurture and care for him through it and to protect him from too much stress. I began to see that when the disease eats away at his body, I also suffer and must find ways to deal honestly with my loss even as I care for him.

It was only in this light—both of us sharing our deepest fears, loss, and struggles—that we were able to begin unraveling the last four years.

As Milton had begun to lose physical strength and vitality, he became increasingly afraid he couldn't meet me, provide for me, protect me. As for me, I saw him shrink back. More important, I felt him shrink back. At the same time, the opening—which we both agreed was from the Lord—came for me to go to Sudan. I stepped forward.

Both of us wanted to be faithful. Obedient. Neither of us was prepared for the price we would be asked to pay. It was the perfect storm.

All foul winds came together tearing at the foundation of our relationship. We both had our fears. We both tried to protect the other. We both had good intentions. We both made terrible mistakes that threatened to unravel us.

A Fire Within

Through loving inspection of the structure of our life together, Milton and I are both learning we cannot protect each other from pain, loss of life, or the cost of our faith, but we can recognize when the load has become too heavy to carry alone. And once we found our passion—what God dreamed of when He first formed us in His hands—we could not shut it up. If we try, it burns within us as though consuming our very bones.

Our framework is weathered by the storm of life and choices we've made along the way. By God's grace, we've been given a second chance, again. We're gutting the rotted timbers of our lives and fortifying the palace with strong, straight, and cured cedar.

It's a risky way to live, investing everything you have in one person, one God, one way of life. There's much to lose. After all, we only have so much time, and so much room for error. We will all die one day. Some of us sooner than others. Some of us more tragically than others. But none of us will get through this life without dying. Some of us will not get through life without losing someone we gave our entire heart, body, and soul to. For a time, the loss will seem unbearable. For a time.

Those of us who wake up longing to know more than the rote answers our culture gives us—who long to recapture that dream God first held as He formed us in His hands—will indeed risk all to live that dream, be that dream.

Here, with our hearts beating wildly, taking stock of all that is at stake, we consider the risk of loss, including life itself. Our bodies wane, weaken, and prepare to die even as we hope against all hope. Clinging to the truth of the resurrection, we throw off our fears and jump into the fray of life holding nothing of ourselves back. Here, in the unavoidable tussle of life and death, the dance floor opens for us to place our hand in His, trust in His lead, and sway in the adoring arms of our Great Lover, our God.

Chapter 23

THE ROAD TO RESTORATION

Few people know the path Milton and I have walked, but when they hear of it, they often ask me, "Are you angry?"

It's a great question, because the first step on the long and winding road to restoration is forgiveness—both giving and receiving. My answer is not an easy one. In truth, I have searched my heart and find no anger for the Muslim men who beat and raped me. They were birthed into evil; they were raised and have lived the whole of their lives in the evil of war, genocide, slavery, and things you, nor I, with our blue passports can even begin to comprehend.

If you are a child watching and experiencing this sort of evil from conception—without knowing the Light of Christ—how it must warp your heart, soul, and mind.

It was easy, even as the violence was unleashed upon me, to forgive those men.

What is harder for me to reconcile is the fact that we American Christians, steeped in every golden opportunity, and most important, the Light of Christ, still don't want to hear, face, and respond to this dark and ever-present reality for the women and children, whom I now rank among.

I find myself wondering, *Where are hell's gate stormers?*

The thought of receiving comfort or empathy from the church leaves me unsettled, when I know there are babies far more vulnerable than me, with no blanket of love rushing to warm their frozen hearts.

I feel so torn, knowing that to stop the cycle of evil we must tend to the abused and abandoned orphan before he becomes the next generation of evildoer.

Today, as I consider all God has done in and through my life, I find regret simply impossible. Hundreds of orphans are alive, happy, and well cared for in some of the darkest corners of our planet all because of God's work through Make Way Partners.

Yes, I've made costly mistakes, but they haven't stopped God. In fact, He has used them to deepen all aspects of my life from my faith to my marriage to how I approach ministry.

The fast-paced fray of leading a growing ministry may have served the good of others much more than my corporate life had, but it had become no less threatening to my own heart.

To heal from the years of piled-up pain and rediscover the lost dream God had for me, the first step toward healing was to admit my desperate need. The second step was to make space for Christ to come to me in my desperation, through Milton and others. *Make way for the coming of the Lord.*

I began by letting go of my daily checklist of things that I thought had to be accomplished within a certain time frame. Instead of starting my day by launching into that rote list, I made an intentional choice to carve out room for what my heart required. To fortify my heart, I stayed in my journal every day rereading the names He gave me on the mountain.

Most days the words didn't feel real. I tried to remember how I felt when He gave them to me, but often the feelings just weren't there. I had to go by what I knew was truth rather than how I felt. This affirmed why it had been so important to write down every detail He gave me on the mountain, so that back down in the valley of life, they were not forgotten, and I was not lost. On days when I couldn't feel the names God gave me, I saw them in tear-stained ink, recorded the very day He showed me how He saw me.

Drawing from His names for me: Gentle One, Confident, Art in Motion, Lover, Beautiful Dancing One, Faithful One, Resurrection, and more, I began to live from those names.

Each day, I found myself crying. Sometimes these tears were for myself, but more often they were for the suffering of the innocent, the state of the world, and how I began to see where God's heart breaks for us all. I'd felt very tender and sorrowful for these things before, but in my energetic response to try to do something to right these wrongs, I'd never really let the full weight of the pain have its proper place in my life.

Allowing my body the freedom to express the beat of my heart was just as important. I made room for dance in my life. Now, at some point every day, I dance. Sometimes these dances are a romantic dance with or for my husband. Other times they are quiet healing prayers sung through the rhythm of my body's movements. I know God hears these prayers because sometimes I feel Him respond by moving my body to His own rhythms. I am dancing with God.

Each day, there are still certain responsibilities I must meet: family; home; friends; lectures; staff needs; working with our indigenous leaders in Sudan, Congo, and Romania; donor relations; administrative requirements; and writing. The difference now is I no longer answer these needs as if the world will fall apart if I am unable to meet them.

I still have to remind myself daily: If God's grace was sufficient for Paul and is sufficient for me, then it must surely be sufficient for those asking things of me as well. Sometimes I have to say, "I'm sorry. I can do no more today." Then I dance or cry—or both—until I begin to fill with life again.

I've been a Christian for more than four decades. I've spent most of my days filling up those decades living from a list of things to do or not do. As I studied Scripture through the years, my understanding of what I should be doing grew, and thus the things on my list became clearer each year. But most of the good things came from my understanding of what made up a good Christian life; they did not flow from my heart.

The more attuned to my heart—and honest with others about it—I became, the more life's tussle intensified, especially at home. There is no more intimate, demanding, or complex relationship than that between a husband and his wife. I am married to a good husband. The fact that he is my husband means he is a man, which means he is a human. I, too, am human, and that combination makes a foolproof recipe for hurt.

Hiding, for a time, deep in our own storm shelters, we each began to dig up the roots of pain, loss, anger, and fear that threatened to choke the life out of us. If there is a pretty way to uproot ugliness, neither Milton nor I knew of it, and neither did my therapist.

Along with the crying and dancing, there were many hard confrontations and many hours, days, and weeks of long-buried, heart-wrenching honesty, which was painful for both of us.

At times we could humbly admit our own sin, struggles, and mere humanity—complete with limited understanding—and lavish mercy on each other. At other times, we seemed bent on becoming a personal holy spirit for the other, pointing fingers to ensure the other saw their sin.

After one such difficult confrontation, I retreated to the shower telling myself I had to get ready for work. Tears flowed and mingled with the hot water coursing over my body until I crouched near the floor in sobs. I looked up and saw Milton had opened the shower door; he stood motionless watching me. I wasn't sure how to read his face.

How do two people—good people, Christians committed to God and their faith, who've loved each other and shared life for over twenty years—suddenly find themselves blown miles apart?

I raised myself and stood naked before him, dripping both water and tears.

Still uncertain of the look in his eyes but with sudden personal clarity I risked saying, "I need you. I am so afraid of losing you I'm afraid to really feel that need of you. As you suffer one more consequence or side effect from your diabetes, I feel it is taking you away from me one agonizing day at a time. When you're angry, harsh, or judgmental with me, it feels like I'm losing yet another piece of you. I feel overwhelmed with feelings to run away from it all. But I choose to stay. I choose to admit I love you and am desperate for us—our intimacy. I miss you. I miss our closeness. I want to face and fight whatever lie, sin, issue, disease, or even death we must in order to rebuild the home of our union in the aftermath of this hell storm."

I'm really not sure if Milton pulled me into his bath-robed arms or if I jumped into them, but either way that is where I landed. His sobs let me know the wall of anger was down, and he was as broken as I was.

"Kimberly, you're the ultimate Daughter of Thunder, fiery and passionate. You're so hungry for every breath of life, and so fiercely independent. Oftentimes I'm afraid you run out so far ahead of everyone and everything that you leave yourself vulnerable and will get yourself killed. You want so much out of life … out of me. Sometimes, especially as I don't have the stamina I had before, I'm so afraid I cannot meet you there. Cannot give you what you want or need. I'm sad because—out of that fear—a part of me just gave up. Just quit trying. I hid too. Forgive me. I'm so sorry. I don't want to lose you. I love you more than life itself, but I have let fear keep me from showing you—giving you—my best love. Forgive me, my love; I don't want to lose any part of you. We're all dying, but I know my disease is quickly taking its toll on me. Whether we have one, ten, or twenty years left together, I don't want to let fear come between us any longer."

Under the covers seemed to be the safest place to let our broken hearts heal. Lying in bed many long hours, we shared our hearts in the safety of each other's arms. We let God show us exactly how we'd both been trying to protect each other from things that we were probably more afraid of than the other would've been. He showed us our sin; He gave us His grace, mercy, and yes, a second chance.

I hid what happened to me in Sudan out of apprehension that Milton would try to stop me from returning there, fear of the deathly toll sharing in my suffering might take on him, and most of all, shame. Milton hid his fear that age and diabetes had stolen so much from him that he could no longer meet me where I wanted him, needed him.

In each other's arms we could both see the lies that threatened to take us out. Through transparency, it became clear that all either of us wanted was to be and to have the loving mate God intended when He first dreamed of Milton and Kimberly L. Smith. By accepting both our joy and sorrow, we're becoming just that.

Milton, too, is growing and finally tasting morsels of the rich life of meaning he hungered for so many years ago. He knows his love for me saved my life, and he knows he makes a difference in the world every single day. Sometimes it might be more than he bargained for, but he says he wouldn't change the journey, or me, for anything in the world.

Like Adam and Eve, God called us both from the bush of our hiding places. I've never regretted answering His call to come out. It may sound strange, but while I was working so hard to hide my failure and sin, I was such a slave to shame. Paradoxically, once I took the very action I was most certain would tear down everything I'd worked so hard to achieve—reveal my failure, sin, and suffering—shame lost its lien against me. Instead of condemnation, I felt free for the first time in many years.

FROM MY HEART TO YOURS

Finally, I've found exactly what I was created to be and do. I have no doubt I am married to the man I need to be married to and I am up to my neck in the exact Kingdom role I was designed to play. My daily prayer is that God would use my victories, wounds, and transgressions forged along the way to encourage others to risk losing everything to know the life God dreams for them, for you.

I pray my journey helps you to discover—then dare to uncover—whatever shame, fear, or lies Satan uses to keep you bound and barred from living the life God dreams for you.

This is life on the edge—where so much is uncertain, maybe even scary, certainly out of our control; but it's also where true freedom lives.

Alcoholics Anonymous has a saying: "Yesterday is history; tomorrow's a mystery." The space in between is as thin and sharp as a razor. It's called today. Steadying ourselves on today demands neither regretting nor glorifying yesterday, while not attempting to control what tomorrow may bring. Living today requires a sense of adventure, engaging both the joy and the sorrow, the beauty and the pain of every moment of every day, and searching for God's dry stones in the turbulent waters of life.

When we're willing to do that, it doesn't matter if we find ourselves in the Sahara Desert, an urban jungle, or our own family circus, the fog clears and we begin to see who He imagined when He first dreamed of us. Your journey will sail you through different ports than mine, but it will most assuredly be full of your own

God-ordained adventures. Largely, if you let it, it will lead you to face some of your deepest fears.

Your journey will be where God's pleasure and your purpose meet, not mine. Your destination is the same as mine—an intimate encounter between you and your Creator—but your route will be filled with adventures, both mild and wild, made just for you.

No less challenging.

No less exhilarating.

Uniquely yours.

As when Abraham placed Isaac on the altar, when we're ready to risk what we hold most sacred, we step into that adventurous life, the only one that matters. There we find our purpose and feel His pleasure—His delight in us. Beaming with the Light of His image, we clearly see the exact dream He holds for each one of us. In that Light and life, we find Him—our passport through darkness.

Love,
your sister along the journey,

k

RECOMMENDED
RESOURCES

Hopefully *Passport through Darkness* has whetted your appetite for finding your specific role in Kingdom work. Below are the websites to a few great organizations that are referenced in the book and that may be helpful conduits for living out what God created you to be and do. Any of them are worthy of your support. In the same world in which many of us drop five dollars a day for a latte grande, one dollar per day can feed a child who would otherwise not eat at all.

Make Way Partners: www.makewaypartners.org
BethanyKids: www.bethanykids.org
The Voice of the Martyrs: www.persecution.com
Africa Inland Mission: http://aimair.org
African Leadership: www.africanleadership.org

For additional reading on the slave trade and what we should do about it, check out these books:

Not for Sale by David Batstone
Scars and Stilettos by Harmony Dust
The Sacred Bath by Theresa L. Flores
The Hole in the Gospel: What Does God Expect of Us? by Richard Stearns

Discover More Online

KimberlyLSmith.com